DEANSGATE

Deansgate, the way to the Dene (valley) and Deane Moor of yesteryear, and the scene of much fighting and bloodshed during the third and final assault on Bolton by Royalist forces in May, 1644, is one of the three oldest roads in Bolton town centre. Yet it is only over the last 100 years that the thoroughfare has developed into the major shopping and commercial area that we know today.

100 years ago there were 26 public houses along the street. Today there are only seven. The gradual whittling down of these hostelries has resulted in their sites being gobbled up by private enterprise. Major banking concerns have set up cheek by jowl with local tradesmen and, as the town grew, so the multiple and major stores realised the advantages of Deansgate as a "High Street" and consequently moved in.

St Paul's Church

Standing like a sentinel over the west end of Deansgate and the convergence of several thoroughfares, St Paul's Church also keeps a watchful and benevolent eye on the Moor Lane and Spa Road (Spaw Lane) areas. At the time of its consecration in 1865 the population of the Parish was 7,000, but the sweeping away of housing properties in the Spring Gardens/Howell Croft area

for
Ce
for
num

ama
Paul's with that of Emmanuel created a new parish of some 12,000 people and more recently housing development alongside Moor Lane has helped to swell this figure.

White Lion, Gipsy's Tent, Ritherdon's, Navada

Whilst the church attends to the spiritual needs of its parishioners the two nearby public houses, the White Lion and the Gipsy's Tent have, over a considerable number of years, attended to the needs of the inner man. Research has attempted to ascertain how the Gipsy's Tent obtained its somewhat unusual name. The only logical conclusion is that the hostelry was built on or

Deansgate in the 1890s. Note the predominantly dark suits and dresses of the pedestrians, and the tall figure of Britannia atop Constantine's, later Woolworth's premises. From the impressively named and imposing Williams Deacon's and Manchester and Salford Bank Ltd., at the corner of Market Street, were Reynolds', fruiterers; Higson's, ironmongers; Graveson's, ironmongers, symbolised by the giant lock; Stead and Simpson, boot and shoe manufacturers (today in the Arndale Centre); the Rope and Anchor; Fleming Reid and Co., hosiery manufacturers; John Whitaker, draper and, on the corner of Bridge Street, either Mrs Whitehead's confectioners or Cash's boot and shoe manufacturers. The Rope and Anchor closed in 1899 and, along with Fleming's, Whitaker's and another shop, was demolished in 1900 for the widening of Bridge Street. Not a mechanical vehicle in sight. The age of mechanisation in the form of electric trams was still to dawn and horse trams operated over the single track. In the distance can be seen the Churchgate cab shelter. This was eventually removed in 1908 because of its then dirty and neglected condition. 12 months later the present market cross was erected thereabouts.

near to the site of a gipsy's or a fortune teller's tent.

At the rear of the Gipsy's Tent is Salt Pie Yard. Salt Pie or "sawt Pie" was the old name for a salt box, and back-to-back cottages which once occupied the site were known by that name in the Lancashire vernacular of Victorian days. Here the firm of Ritherdon's, electro-platers and enamellers, occupied the old North Bridge Mill for over 40 years until they removed to Lorne Street, Darwen, in the 1940s. Percy Ritherdon, founder of the firm, was a conjuring enthusiast and no mean exponent of the art. Many were the illusions made at the mill by Mr Ritherdon and his dedicated team and the works provided tricks and equipment for all the great conjurers and illusionists of the day. Names like Carlton, Carl Hertz, De Biere, Carno, Dr Bodie, Margo, Horace Goldin, P T Selbitt, Maskelyne and Devant, Colpitt, the Great Levante and Lafayette spring to mind.

The firm's principal customer, however, was Chung Ling Soo, world famous illusionist William Ellsworth Robinson. Mystery still surrounds Soo's death at the Wood Green Empire in 1918, when he was fatally shot while performing his bullet catching trick. The great illusionist used 20 tons of props in his act, and it is said that at one time he had 2,000 tons of equipment spread over various storage places throughout the country. A considerable amount was stored at the North Bridge Mill and several years after his death it took a 22-ton railway truck to move it to the home of another illusionist.

During the latter half of the last century the area at the rear of the Gipsy's Tent was frequently visited by a travelling dentist, who extract-ed teeth to the accompaniment of a band. Apparently, the shouts and screams of his patients were drowned by the music played by his enthus-iastic musicians.

At the junction of Spa Road and White Lion Brow the building which now houses the Navada roller skating rink and dance hall began its life as the Olympia roller skating rink in September, 1909. This closed early in 1912 and, on May 27th of that year, became the Olympia picture house. The Olympia became the Regal Cinema on September 16th, 1929, and this in turn changed its name to the Astor Cinema on Nov-

ember 24th, 1952. After 43 years as a cinema the building reverted to a roller skating rink with the open-ing of the Navada in November, 1955.

Nearby property, once used as an old grain store, took on a com-pletely new life in December, 1978, when Crompton's Mule Bistro opened therein, followed six months later by a restaurant.

Marsden Road

Marsden Road, popularly known as "T'High Level", connects Deans-gate with St George's Road and was officially opened in May, 1877, by Alderman Peter Crook Marsden (d.1913), whose name it bears. It replaced steep descents to the Croal, the latter being crossed hereabouts by an old wooden bridge set on stones. A curious fact about the present-day road that is not gener-ally known is that it is built in three sections. Bark Street is crossed by an iron girder bridge, St Helena Road by a "skew" bridge of stone and brick and the River Croal by a brick arch.

From the road's inception the idea was to erect shops on each side of it, and a writer in the Bolton Weekly Journal on the day it was officially opened stated that "The timber fencing which extends the entire length of the road is only in-tended as a temporary hoarding, which will be removed as soon as shops are erected on each side of the road, ample building plots be-ing now vacant for that purpose."

The intention to have shops alongside the road was not merely for appearance sake. Having pur-chased considerable land and prop-erty to make way for the High Level, our Victorian predecessors were under the impression that they could, at a later date, reimburse themselves by selling this land for shops. They possibly had not real-ised at the time the cost of building up to the Marsden Road level. In fact, a suggestion in 1936 that the fire station should be extended along the road brought a storm of protest when it was realised that of the £37,000 estimated for such an extension £15,000 would be needed to bring the fire station up to the road level. No shops were ever built and the wooden fences remain-ed for 67 years until 1944, when they were taken down and replaced by brick walls.

An "institution" since 1867 (in

May of that year, a beginning was made in premises in Tipping Street to teach some useful trade to blind men and women) the Workshops of the Blind in Marsden Road were opened in May, 1914. Nine years ago they opened their doors to all disabled people and changed their title to Bolton Industries for the Disabled. They were closed in 1980 on the opening of Bolmoor, a new purpose-built workshop for the blind and disabled on St Helens Road.

On the opposite side of the road the former Bolton Borough Lighting Department offices stand alongside the thoroughfare like part of the superstructure of a giant merchant ship. In days gone by a glance over the wall to the yard below revealed a forest of old gas and electricity lamp standards, each one waiting either to be sold as scrap or to enjoy a prolonged life in a private drive or garden.

Today, the phased traffic signals at the Deansgate/Marsden Road junction occasionally cause con-fusion but during the 50s and part of the 60s the roundabout and is-lands thereabouts were colloquially known as the "S(c)illy Isles" be-cause of the chaos frequently caused by their very existence. They were removed in 1964 when the traffic lights came into operation.

Fire Station

From 1802 until 1867 Bolton's fire station occupied a ramshackle building adjoining the old lock-up in Old Hall Street. In the latter year a move was made to more commodious premises in Coronation Street but these were soon consider-ed inadequate and, as it was thought desirable to provide living accommodation for permanent staff, the impressive building sweeping along-side Marsden Road to the Deansgate corner and on to St Edmund Street was opened in October, 1899, on the site of the old Fox and Goose beerhouse. Consequently, on one December day 14 years later, ped-estrians on Deansgate and Bradshaw-gate were thrilled to see the first motor fire engine, an 85h.p. Leyland, career along to its first fire at a speed that even surprised the police officers on point duty. Horses, how-ever, continued to be used until 1916, by which time two petrol-engined machines had been deliver-ed.

The station remained in use until

the opening of the present headquarters on Moor Lane in February, 1971. The old building, now known as Marsden House, is occupied by Bolton Metropolitan Borough Social Services Department. From the 1920s until comparatively recent times successive cleaning firms - Metro Co., Beau Brummel Ltd. and Allens - occupied the ground floor premises in that part of the old fire station building fronting Deansgate. Youngsters particularly used to be fascinated by the operation of the giant steam press which was positioned facing the large window.

50 years ago Gordons, authorised Ford dealers, had premises next to the cleaners at the corner of St Edmund Street.

St Edmund Street

St Edmund Street, during most of the 19th century known as Grime Street after a Mr Grime who had a shop there at the beginning of the century, owes its present name to the Roman Catholic Church which now presides over it. From writings at the time of laying foundation stones, opening ceremonies and the like, much can be gleaned of contemporary social conditions. The stone-laying ceremony for St Edmund's in 1860 was no exception.

Speeches made on the occasion establish that the new church was set in an area particularly occupied by the lowest and most disreputable characters of the town. Canon Carter, who was given the dual task of setting up two new missions, the parishes of St Patrick's and St Edmund's, had also been given the option of the site now occupied by St Paul's Church, but he chose Grime Street "so that the poor, humble people of the new parish would be enabled to slip in and out of their church unobtrusively in their clogs and shawls." A noble gesture and obviously one much appreciated, because the parish thrived and the church is still going strong after 121 years. The adjacent junior school was closed in 1962.

The bridge over the Croal at the bottom of the street was inaugurated by Alderman Miles, Mayor of Bolton 1901-3, in 1902. At its right hand corner with Deansgate, the building which is now a D.I.Y. decorating materials store has had various occupiers over the past 50 years, including Pilkington, motor engineer; a Tognarelli's cafe; Holroyd's cycles; King's, scooters and motor cycles; and a carpet store.

Deansgate Warehouse

It is 19 years since the tall warehouse adjoining the White Lion was demolished. Baines' 1824 map of Bolton shows a branch "rail road" in existence, starting from premises on Deansgate and linking up with an intended "rail road" at Lecturer's Close (presumably the Bolton-Leigh line opened in August 1828). In his booklet "The Railways of Bolton 1824-1959" J R Bardsley points out that "The history of the branch line to Deansgate is of considerable interest. It crossed Crook Street, Great Moor Street and New Street by means of level crossings and ended at the goods warehouse on Deansgate...For many years the steel works, which occupied a large site bounded by Moor Lane...kept the branch railway busy. The engines which hauled the trains and wagons to and from the Forge, as it was always known, were fitted with a bell to give warning of their approach. The works ceased production in 1924 and were subsequently dismantled, and with them went the branch railway; the L.N.W.R. had stopped using the Deansgate warehouse at some time previous to this."

The warehouse was then leased by Bolton Corporation to Harry Mason and Sons Ltd. The firm moved out in 1962 and the building was demolished the following year. Its site is now a pleasant garden retreat where seats beckon the weary to rest their aching limbs. This, however, will again be transformed

in the not too distant future. Bolton's new £4,000,000 Crown Court complex at its rear opened in March 1982 and ultimately, after demolition of the block of property at the junction of Blackhorse Street and Deansgate, the site of the warehouse will be landscaped to provide an appropriate setting for the prestigious building.

Blackhorse Street

Two centuries ago Blackhorse Street was known as Thweat Street after James Thweat (Thwaites or Twaites) who is reputed to have built Bolton's first spinning mill in King Street in 1780. The street took its present title from the Black Horse Inn, formerly sited on the east side of the thoroughfare just round the corner from Deansgate, which closed in 1937. The hostelry was the first Bolton residence of Isaac Dobson and later the headquarters of the Black Horse Club, comprising mainly prominent local industrialists and founded by Isaac and Benjamin Dobson, Peter Rothwell and Benjamin Hick. This Club was instrumental in securing for Samuel Crompton in his later years an annuity of £63-15-0d.

In 1790 Isaac Dobson and Peter Rothwell founded a textile machinery firm in Blackhorse Street which, through a succession of owners and titles - Isaac and Benjamin Dobson; executors of the late Benjamin Dobson; Dobson and Metcalf; Dobson and Barlow (1850-1970); Platt International Ltd. (1970-75) - and

The former Black Horse Hotel from which Blackhorse Street takes its name

two subsequent moves became the world-renowned textile machinery manufacturing company of Platt Sacco-Lowell Ltd., Bradley Fold. This, apart from the foundry and the sheet metal operation, closed in December 1981.

The old works originally fronted Blackhorse Street from near Barn Street (perpetuating Barn Meadow and Higher Meadow, a rural simplicity of two centuries ago) to the present Cheadle Square. In 1832 Benjamin Dobson more than doubled the area of the works after the purchase of a large plot of land between Queen Street and Blackhorse Street, today occupied by Cheadle Square and gardens. This cost him £3,660. In 1931 the works and machinery on this site, then owned by W and E Rigby Ltd., engineers and calendar bowl makers, Queen's Foundry, was purchased by Bolton Corporation for £50,000.

Little remains of the original frontage to Blackhorse Street, only the old works entrance and a stretch of wall adjoining the former Bolton ambulance headquarters at the corner of Cheadle Square. The building which until recently housed the town's ambulance service stands on part of Dobson and Rothwell's works, and replaced previous premises destroyed by fire in 1895. The ambulance station was closed in April,

Looking out over the Moor Lane – New Street junction in 1925. The proliferation of chimneys belonged to Bessemers Ltd., steel manufacturers. The site had been completely cleared by early 1927 and in 1930 Moor Lane bus station came into use on part of it. The present wholesale and retail markets were opened in September, 1932

1978, following the transfer of its ambulances to the new control centre at Farnworth.

The street also has a strong connection with the present Hick, Hargreaves and Co. Ltd. After his apprenticeship at Leeds, Benjamin Hick joined the Union Foundry,

Moor Lane/Blackhorse Street, whose owners became Messrs Rothwell, Hick and Rothwell. Later, in 1833, Benjamin Hick established his own business at Crook Street in partnership with his two young sons.

Industrial archaeologists will be interested in the description of the

A busy Moor Lane bus station during Bolton Holidays in July, 1939, only two months before the clouds of war rolled over. Service buses and coaches line up to take passengers to their destinations, while the adjoining fair waits for its customers.

A photograph taken today from the same spot as this one would necessitate standing in the centre of a busy roadway and looking up a considerably widened Blackhorse Street. Both the King's Head Hotel and Kate Wright's confectioners shop are no longer with us. Blackhorse Street appears at the extreme right of the picture.

Union Foundry which appeared in "Iron" (1873) - "Situated in Blackhorse Street, Bolton-le-Moors, and immediately adjacent to the Bolton Iron and Steel Works...we find one of the oldest engineering works in Lancashire, which may fairly claim to vie with any of its kindred, whether predecessors, contemporaries, or successors, in respect of the quality and magnitude of its productions. The Union Foundry of Messrs Rothwell & Co. is confidently stated to have been the first industrial establishment of the kind found in Bolton, and thus may be accounted, so to say, as the parent and antetype of the numerous other works of the same description that, at the present day, constitute thriving elements in the prosperity of the place. This foundry has been in existence for well nigh a century ..."

Later Rothwell's went out of business and their works was swallowed up by the Bolton Iron and Steel Co., which subsequently became Bessemer's Foundry. The whole area was completely cleared by early 1927; in December 1930 the Moor Lane bus station came into being on part of it and, two years later, the new wholesale market on another part.

Cheadle Square

Between Blackhorse Street and Le Mans Crescent lies Cheadle Square, named after the late Councillor Frank Cheadle (d.1940) who,

for many years before his death, had suggested that space should be allocated at the rear of the Crescent for a garden to provide some refuge in an otherwise dull town centre.

Shortly after the plot of land between Queen Street and Blackhorse Street had been laid out as a garden in 1947, the Highways

Committee deferred a decision to name the area "Civic Gardens". Subsequently Bolton Town Council, at its meeting on September 4th, 1947, decided that the street from the archway to Blackhorse Street should be known as "Cheadle Square" in memory of Councillor Cheadle.

Hen and Chickens, King's Head Hotel

For years Greenall Whitley's (earlier Magee's) Hen and Chickens and Walker's (earlier Tong's) King's Head Hotel stood side by side. This alliance was to end in 1969, when the latter was demolished to make way for the reconstruction and widening of Blackhorse Street.

The Hippodrome

On the other side of the Hen and Chickens stood the Hippodrome Theatre, the home for years of repertory. Opened in 1908 as a variety theatre, many famous show business people trod its stage over the succeeding years - among them Vesta Tilley, Sir Seymour Hicks, Bransby Williams and Gracie Fields. In September, 1923, the Hippodrome opened as a cinema and continued as such until 1940, when the Lawrence Williamson Repertory Players took over and, from 1959, the Bolton Repertory Players. Closed in

The Hippodrome Theatre looking somewhat woebegone six years before its demolition in 1968. After 21 years of repertory and 1,107 different productions the last play there, "The First Mrs Fraser", was presented on July 29th 1961, and the final cast for all time comprised Geoffrey Tetlow, Leslie Ward, Hugh Wallington, Olive Kilner, Dennis Tynsley, Colin Wilson, Alison Ross and Dorina Brown.

1961, the building was demolished in 1968 and the Deansgate Health Centre opened on its site in January, 1972.

Queen Street

100 years ago Queen Street, named in honour of Queen Charlotte, wife of George III, was a cul-de-sac which led into the yard of the Blackhorse Street Machine Works and to the rear of a cotton mill. Nevertheless, its short length included two public houses, the Queen's Arms and the Queen Street Tavern, and a Ragged School. The Ragged School was subsequently incorporated into the Queen Street Mission and the two public houses have long since disappeared. Today, Queen Street is over three times as long as its predecessor and, passing along the rear of Le Mans Crescent, joins Deansgate with Ashburner Street. However, only three properties actually front on to the street, a printers, probation office (formerly Bolton Welfare Department) and the Deansgate Health Centre.

King Street

King Street, on the opposite side of Deansgate, was named after George III (1738-1820), whose 60-years' reign marked one of the greatest periods in British history, although he himself was a controversial figure. To Boltonians particularly, the street will always be associated with the town's famous son, Samuel Crompton, who lived there from about 1800 until his death in 1827. Whether at 15 or 17 there is some doubt, but in any case the argument as to which one is now purely hypothetical as both properties were demolished in 1973.

Crompton also rented other property in the street and, it is said, the top floor of a nearby factory which has been owned by Messrs John Booth and Sons since 1894. For many years a board affixed to the roof facing Marsden Road announced that "In this ancient mill Samuel Crompton first worked his spinning mule 1800" and Crompton's tenancy is apparently mentioned in the mill deeds. The attic room in which he worked is no longer in existence but during the Samuel Crompton Centenary celebrations in 1927 it was visited by over 15,000 people.

St Helena Mill, St Helena Road

Across the Croal in St Helena Road proudly stands the St Helena Mill, formerly owned by Robert Walker Ltd. Up to its closure at the end of 1979 it claimed to be the oldest mill operating in Bolton. Its last owners also believed that at one time Samuel Crompton worked on his spinning mule at the mill.

Deeds, yellowing with age, show that in 1777 a Joseph Blundell, who presumably gave his name to the nearby Blundell Street, leased land on which most of the mill now stands, the idea being to erect a mill on it. By 1781 the property was obviously in existence, for in that year it was held by executors of James Thweat (Thwaites or Twaites). Presumably it was owned earlier by James Thweat himself and this, coupled with other factors, strongly suggests that it was the first spinning mill in Bolton erected "at the bottom of King Street" by James Thwaites in 1780. Eventually the mill was purchased by Roger Walker, then in 1839 by Robert Walker; in 1906 it became a limited company.

Why St Helena Mill? Introduced in the 19th century, the name is linked with Napoleon's exile on the island of St Helena. In its earliest years the mill machinery was powered by a water wheel. To operate this system the buildings were surrounded by a goit, leaving them on what appeared to be an island. It is said that because of this a relative of Walkers who had fought at Waterloo named the mill St Helena Mill. Later, St Anthony Street became St Helena Road.

Post Office, Telecommunications Department

Although Bolton's postal business had been conducted for most of the 18th century at the Bird i'th'Hand public house in Bank Street, the first person to be designated as postmaster was one James Preston, who began a post office at his chemist's and druggist's shop in Deansgate about 1789. Business was later transferred to the Bradshawgate/Wood Street corner (c1818) and from there to the Old Market Square in 1857. Subsequently, a move was made to more commodious premises at the Bradshawgate/Silverwell Street corner in 1868.

As the volume of business further increased, so this building proved inadequate and larger premises were planned. Construction of these began on the north side of Deansgate in 1913, on a site that had earlier been occupied by Messrs Bennis iron-founders, cottages, shops and two public houses - the Beehive and the Welcome Home. Because of the threat of war, building was delayed and it was not until November 20th, 1916, that the impressive building fronting Deansgate was opened as Bolton's Head Post Office. This was to close in November, 1969, when a move was made to the newly constructed Victoria House, later Paderborn House, at the corner of Howell Croft North and Victoria Square.

The huge green and white telephone and telecommunications building which dominates the area at the rear of the former Head Post Office opened on January 18th, 1961. On this date Bolton changed over to the Subscriber Trunk Dialling system and became the first town in Lancashire to be converted from manual to STD in one step.

Kingsgate to Central Street

Those changes which have taken place in the shops in the block between Kingsgate and Central Street over the past 30 years reflect, in microcosm, those which are constantly taking place throughout the town generally, particularly with regard to what can be termed the smaller businesses.

In 1949 the line-up comprised Schofield's, paints; Kent's, dress fabrics; the old-established Pare and Co. Ltd., chemist; the Regent, milliners and clothiers, with Jones, hair stylist, above. The showroom of Walter Bradley Ltd., automobile engineers, stood at the corner of Central Street. 10 years later Schofields was still there with next to it Sugden's, outfitters (earlier in Market Street); Pare's, chemist; Young's, confectioners, with Jones's still above and the Lancashire Wallpaper Co. on the corner. The last named had moved to the substantial premises in 1957 after it had been compelled to leave Victoria Square South.

By the beginning of 1968 Schofields had been replaced by Leyland Paints. Sugdens was still there. Next door to the outfitters was Manor/Hughes, photographers/chemist; then Young's and then Crown Wallpapers. At the time of writing SupaSnaps occupy the Kingsgate corner, Whittakers Shoemakers (established 1923) took over the next-door-but-one shop in September, 1971, and in 1980 acquired the adjoining Sugden's shop. Before purchase by Whittakers this had been tenanted by Diana Ross, ladies' and children's wear, and by a fashion shop which catered "for the Fuller Figure". In June, 1978, Cane Country took over the premises previously owned by Young's, confectioners, and a new hairdressing establishment had taken over from Jones's. Hitchen's clearance store has occupied the corner premises for several years.

During the 17th and 18th centuries particularly Bolton was a major centre for the marketing of fustian – a coarse cotton fabric – and as recently as 1932 the Bolton Directory lists one Fustian Manufacturer in its classified section. This was Dewhirst & Co., 112, Deansgate, premises now occupied by SupaSnaps. Serving as a kind of trademark, a large loom used to stand in the window of the shop.

Incidentally, there does not appear to be much original fustian about these days. In fact, research has so far revealed none. If a reader has a piece or pieces of 17-19th century fustian (two sets of cotton wefts woven on a linen warp) hidden away in cellar or attic, Bolton Museum will be delighted to receive any identifiable samples. This does not refer to more recent fustian exemplified by a class of heavy cotton fabrics including moleskin, velveteen and corduroy.

Central Street

Central Street was originally

named Water Street after the River Croal which flows along the bottom of it. Later it was considered necessary to alter the name in order to avoid confusion with the street of the same name in Little Bolton. Consequently, a suggestion was made, more than likely in a jocular vein, that it be rechristened Idle Lane "for there are none but idle scamps and vagabonds living there". Whether a joke or not, this derogatory title was given to the street. In 1893 the name was changed again, this time to the present Central Street.

Today, Central Street is best known as the site of what appears to be the inappropriately named Queen Street Mission. This apparent incongruity is easily explained by the fact that the Mission originated as Queen Street Mission in the street of that name 109 years ago and retained its title upon moving to its present premises in 1893.

The old-established hair-dressing business of Washington's has been in its premises at the Deansgate end of the street since the early 1950s and at the bottom of the street the Bolton Hide Skin and Fat Co. Ltd. has carried on its substantial business since the 1890s, when the firm moved from Canal Road, off Church Wharf.

Ask most people, particularly the younger ones, where Mick Buck's Bridge is and they will just look blank. Yet the bridge, which crosses the Croal at the bottom of Central Street, is still frequently

referred to by older residents as Mick Buck's Bridge, even though the original cast iron structure built by M Buck and Sons has been replaced within the last decade by brick and concrete.

Slightly further down the Croal and overlooking it stands the huge Victoria Hall. Its side is well worth looking up (if you will pardon the expression) for its numerous foundation stones, all dated 1898 and presented by the influential people of the day, the areas of numbered bricks subscribed by the not so influential, and the coloured glass windows.

Nearby in Chapel Alley is William Bleasdale and Sons, Central Forge, established in the 1880s and an anachronism in modern times. Velvet Walks, now a car park under that title, implies a once verdant area but at the same time signifies a place where velvets were made.

One of the last relics of the age of Victorian social welfare disappeared in 1979 when the former Kings Gate Institution, Kings Gate/Central Street, built in 1876 as a haven for the poor and down-and-outs, was demolished. It closed as a Casual Ward in the 1940s and had been owned by the G.P.O. since then.

Central Street to Ridgway Gates

The property between Central Street and Ridgway Gates is representative of pre-1900 building in Deansgate. Small compact properties, stepped in height, contrast with more recent and in many cases larger buildings.

At the corner of Central Street the late Douglas Stanley Rowley founded his optical business in 1907. The shop next door to Rowley's, now under the title of the West End News Agency, will always be remembered as housing Winterburn's, booksellers, possibly at the time the best known business in the town. Winterburn's started at the corner of Deansgate and Oxford Street in the early 19th century and moved to 96A, Deansgate, in 1930. John Read (Booksellers) Ltd. took over this firm six years later and in its turn Read's was acquired by W H Smith and Son in 1967.

Like the other remaining public houses in that half of Deansgate, the Blue Boar has seen countless changes during its lengthy existence.

"They don't make 'em like that any more". The stylish and elegant Mick Buck's Bridge which spanned the Croal at the bottom of Central Street

Danger, men at work. Resurfacing the western end of Deansgate in the late 1920s. Note the solid tyred Leyland Leviathan heading for Third Avenue. This service began in July, 1924, and continues today as part of the 511/512 circular service.

One of these was the closure of its near neighbour for many years, the King's Arms, in March, 1962. With the opening of Chapter and Verse, booksellers, there in May, 1974, the premises catered for intellectual needs instead of drinking needs. This usage was to be continued from December, 1980, when the Preston firm of Sweetens, booksellers, opened in the building.

Old maps of Deansgate show a considerable number of open and enclosed alleys and ginnels leading from the thoroughfare to courts and yards at its rear — Bamber Court, Collingwood Court, Millstone Yard, Wood's Court, Duke's Alley, Salt Pie Yard, Cunliffe Court. Central Street itself led to a multiplicity of such courts — Gibbon's, Holden's, Fogg's, Edge's, Oliphant and Albion. Today few alleyways remain. One of them is Chapel Alley, now but a shadow of its former self, passing between the Blue Boar and Greenhalgh's Craft Bakery Shop. Leading in its heyday to the Albion Works and Velvet Walks, it took its name from Duke's Alley Chapel which stood alongside it.

A study of the Bolton directories of 50–60 years ago shows that a considerable number of shops which changed hands around that era were taken over by similar businesses. Today this trend is not so apparent. The scale of commerce and modern shopfitting techniques, coupled with availability of funds, means that any premises can be easily and quickly altered to an entirely dissimilar use to their previous one.

Chapel Alley to Ridgway Gates is a classic example of change of

A bedecked Palatine Street between Ridgway Gates and Knowsley Street on July 7th, 1936. On that particular day His Royal Highness, the Duke of Kent, passed through Bolton on his way to Darwen but neither the bunting nor the assembled throng was there to welcome him. The multitude was just a portion of the large crowd which had gathered outside Horrocks's store for another "Royal" occasion, the arrival of the Cotton Queen.

ownership but not of type of business. In the 1927 Directory Joseph Ratcliffe, florist, was at 92A; by 1932 Spibey, fruiterer and florist, had taken over and for 38 years until June, 1981, the extended premises were The Oxford, fruiterer and florist. Greenhalgh's, baker and confectioners, opened there at the end of January. Next door passed through James Bowker, grocer, a Mrs A Wolstencroft, grocer, to - more recently - Thos. Holt, grocer. The shop is now Gibson's Sports. For many years the grocer's was The Little Shop, a veritable Aladdin's Cave entered down a sloping passageway. It was affectionately referred to as "Ta-Thank You's" on account of the habit of its manageress of thanking each customer for his or her order and subsequently thanking each person again as they left the shop.

On the site of Podmore's in the 19th century stood another of Deansgate's many public houses - the Old Hen and Chickens. This must certainly have caused confusion at times considering that the present Hen and Chickens existed on the other side of the road. However, its licence was eventually removed in 1888 to the Railway Shipping Inn, Crook Street.

Podmore's, previously at 16, Bank Street and earlier in Great Moor Street, took over the premises of William Southern, seed merchants, over 50 years ago. Next door, according to the 1927 Bolton Directory, were Vose and Son, tripe dealers, who later occupied premises near the Oxford Street corner. By the time the 1932 Directory had appeared Mr Tognarelli had opened another of his shops, a confectioner's, in the premises. Subsequently, it was Bullough's cake shop before becoming the present Cheadles.

At 84, Hampson's, the second oldest of the firm's present-day local shops, opened approximately 60 years ago. In June, 1960, the shop was re-opened after renovations which, it was claimed, made it the "most up-to-date confectioner's shop in Lancashire".

After many years the Fleetwood Fish Supply closed its shop at the corner of Ridgway Gates but today the premises still supply food, in this case through a cafe and snack bar.

The rear of this section of Deansgate has been associated both with the founding church for Congregationalism in Bolton and later, for many years, with the Methodist cause. In the first place, this was the Duke's Alley Chapel and in the second, Methodism has flourished here for over 200 years, through the Ridgway Gates Chapel and today through its successors, the Victoria Hall and the Walker Memorial Hall.

In 1754, on a site where earlier George Whitefield had preached, Duke's Alley Chapel was opened as the first Independent (later Congregational) Chapel in Bolton. Earlier a schism had been produced by a breakaway Calvinistic group from Bolton's first Methodist preaching house built adjacent to Hotel Street in 1751, partly because of a dispute over the deeds. The breakaway group was later joined by a considerable number of persons who seceded from the Bank Street Chapel because of the Unitarian tendencies of its minister. Duke's Alley Chapel came into being and for over 150 years it and its successor were faithfully to serve the Congregationists' cause until the building was purchased by the Presbyterian Church of Wales in 1906. Their first service was held in the renovated building, the Welsh Tabernacle, in January, 1908. Bolton Corporation purchased the Tabernacle in 1960 and the building was demolished in 1968. Its site is now a Corporation car park.

Between 1748 and 1790 the great John Wesley preached in Bolton on numerous occasions and it was therefore most fitting that, when the Methodist meeting house in Hotel Street became too small to accommodate all those who wished to attend it and a new larger chapel was built at Ridgway Gates, Wesley should be asked to open it. This he did, on April 16th, 1776, and so the Ridgway Gates Chapel came into existence within a stone's throw of the breakaway Duke's Alley Chapel. Wesley called the Ridgway Gates Chapel "One of the most elegant houses in the Kingdom" and "the lovely house at Bolton".

The last service in the old Chapel was held in March, 1900, consequent on the opening of the Victoria Hall. Thereafter the building served several ecclesiastical purposes before it was eventually demolished in 1931 and on its site was built the Walker Memorial Hall, opened the following year.

Ridgway Gates

Ridgway Gates (today spelt differently on each side of the thoroughfare) takes its name from James Ridgway, dyer and bleacher, who once owned much property thereabouts. His name appears on an auction advertisement in 1778 as "in possession of a certain plot, piece, or parcel of land, situate, lying, and being on the North side of Deansgate, hereafter to be called 'Ridgway Street'..." Later the name was changed to Ridgway Gates and the 1953 Bolton Survey confirms that there were actually gates, originally erected to protect Ridgway's bleaching grounds, which lay in the vicinity of the present Market Hall.

Today Ridgway Gates leads principally to the car park of that name, to the Walker Memorial Hall, previously mentioned, and to the large building now a furniture store opened by Wades in January,1981. This was formerly owned by Williams from May, 1978 to October, 1980, and before that by Habitat 1974-78, but is better known as having housed Horrocks (Ridgway Gates) Ltd., furnishers, milliners and soft furnishing, from 1856 until 1974.

Messrs Coombes, shoe repairers, opened in the street in July, 1960, but later moved to premises at the corner with Deansgate. Next door to the present Coombes' shop, Curry's, radio, TV and electrical goods, opened in 1960 and closed in December, 1980, on removal of their business to premises in Newport Street. Recently the Department of the Environment gave the green light for the use of the former Curry's shop as an amusement centre.

Lloyd's Bank Buildings

Lloyd's Bank opened at 127-129 Deansgate in 1924, in premises previously occupied by Mr Tognarelli, motor haulage contractor, char-a-banc proprietor, confectioner, cafe proprietor and ice cream maker. Several years later the present Lloyd's Bank building was erected, like much property thereabouts, on the site of an ancient hostelry, in this case the Hand and Banner, which had closed in 1911. Apparently, the Hand and Banner had at least two principal claims to fame. First, in 1809, it was the venue for the inauguration of the Friendly Ironmoulders Society. Whatever happened to the unfriendly ironmoulders? Secondly, and much earlier, its site had been occupied by the substantial dwelling house of John Okey, a puritan and prominent Boltonian, who died in 1684 and is best remembered today by his gravestone which lies alongside the south wall of the Parish Church. The potted history of his life and his puritanical view of the times in which he lived inscribed upon it make most interesting and entertaining reading:-

"John Okey the servant of God was borne in London 1608 Came into this Towne 1629 Married Mary the daughter of james Crompton of Breightmet 1635 with whom he lived comfortably 20 years & begot 4 sonns & 6 daughters since then he lived sole till the day of his death In his time were many Great Changes & terrible alterations 18 years civill wars in England besides many dreadfull sea fights The Crown or Command of England changed 8 times episcopacy laid aside 14 yeares London burnt by papists & more stately built againe Germany wasted 300 miles 200000 protestants murdered in Ireland by the papists This towne thrice stormed once taken & plundered He went thorow many troubles & divers conditions Found rest joy and happines only in holines the faith fear & loue of God in Jesus

Christ He dyed the 29 of Ap & lieth here buried 1684 Come Lord Jesus o come quickly."

It is presumed that it was John Okey, known to have an interest in a "parcel of land called the Orchard" in Mealhouse Lane, who gave the site at the Deansgate end of the Lane upon which the Nonconformist Chapel was erected in 1672. The building was finally demolished in 1888.

Lloyd's Bank to Queen Street

Just over 75 years ago there were five public houses in the short stretch between Howell Croft and Blackhorse Street. Mention has already been made of the Hand and Banner, the Hen and Chickens and the King's Head. Of the other two, the Coach and Horses at the corner of Back Spring Gardens was compensated in 1907 and demolished to make way for shops. The Queen's Arms at the corner of Queen Street closed shortly afterwards and its premises were subsequently occupied by a Post Office parcels department and later a temporary post office.

Amongst well-established businesses which have disappeared from the block are the butchering firm of Harts; Hawkins, drapers;

Gilbert Taylor, outfitters; Burgons Ltd. and Sharples Ltd. The latter firm was established in Bolton in 1871 and occupied Deansgate premises from 1930 until 1980.

Bolton Y.M.C.A. was inaugurated in January, 1884, and the Deansgate building opened by Lord Leverhulme in October, 1919, was previously the Imperial Hall. No doubt there are still a few amongst us who can recall a "misspent youth" in Riley's Imperial Temperance Billiard Hall.

Howell Croft

Howell Croft, named after the Howell family, prominent mercers and drapers, originally cut across the croft or meadow owned by the family. At one time it joined Deansgate with Great Moor Street but on the opening of the Town Hall in 1873 the property at the building's rear became part of the Town Hall Square, later Victoria Square. The two Howell Crofts and their connecting link ultimately developed into a collection of miscellaneous businesses and three-storey, handloom weavers' cottages. There were also four public houses between Deansgate and Great Moor Street, two of which, the Founders' Arms at the Ashburner Street corner and the Town Hall Tavern, Victoria Square, were demolished to make

Howell Croft North in the days before Paderborn House. Taken in 1959, the photograph shows Betty's sweet shop; H Lee, grocer; Hughes & Co., drapers and household goods, and the Civil Defence headquarters, all of which were demolished in 1968.

way for the Civic Centre. The Junction Inn, which stood at the corner of Spring Gardens and Howell Croft North, closed in 1908 and its site is now part of the police offices. The Flag Hotel at the Great Moor Street corner closed as recently as November, 1970, and was demolished three months later.

Gone is the slum property between Howell Croft and Spring Gardens and more modern property on its site includes Lever Chambers, which has stood prominently at the corner of Ashburner Street for over 50 years, Elizabeth House, which opened to the public in October, 1971, and the Civic Centre, now Le Mans Crescent, construction of which began in 1931; the whole sweep was formally opened by the Earl of Derby in 1939. The Sessions and Police Department had been informally opened in October, 1934, the Public Health Department and the Central Library in 1938. The Museum was opened in October, 1947. Work on this had been discontinued because of the War and, for the opening, exhibits from the now-demolished Chadwick Museum were brought up to the town centre premises.

The first performance at the Octagon Theatre, on November 14th, 1967, was the world premier of Bill Naughton's play "Annie and Fanny". Princess Margaret officially opened the theatre two weeks later. Paderborn House, Howell Croft North, was opened in 1969.

Aspinall's Buildings

Of the recent businesses in the block between Whitakers and Howell Croft the oldest was Ellwood's, the silk shop, which, until closure in 1981, had been there for about 50 years. Other long standing occupiers in the past were Aspinall's, pork butchers; Batten's, glass and china dealers; Smith's, milliners, and Jackson, hatters and boot specialists. Aspinall's gave way to the Bolton Health Food Centre; more recently Peter Pell's, gents outfitters, became Gibson's Sports (opened June, 1980) and Lester's, ladies' fashions – Kitchens Today – and – from June, 1980 – another Whitaker's shop. Lilley and Skinner, previously Cable Shoes, occupied the corner site on which, from 1900-7, was Yorkshire House, owned by Whitakers. From November, 1981, another Whitaker's has been

What a difference 17 years make! Taken in July, 1965, this photograph shows cars parked where the Octagon Theatre now stands. The large building on the far side of Ashburner Street was built as a store for textile and metal waste in 1867. Purchased by Messrs Magee Marshall & Co in 1884, it was converted into a bonded store and demolished in 1969, 12 months before the brewery itself closed. Beyond the building can be seen part of the Howell Croft bus station, which had a busy life between its opening in 1947 and its closure in 1969. At the top right of Howell Croft, at its junction with Great Moor Street, stands the Flag Hotel. This took its name from a giant flagstone 15 feet square and weighing six tons which covered part of the floor of the hostelry. The public house closed in November, 1970, and was demolished three months later.

in the premises.

Aspinall's was originally founded by the late Edmund Aspinall (d. 1940), former Mayor and Freeman of Bolton, in Folds Road. In 1884 he took the Deansgate premises on a 14-years' lease. Business obviously thrived, for two years before the lease expired he was able to purchase the premises and later, in 1912, he rebuilt his shop and property adjoining, and constructed the Aspin Hall, the whole block being designated Aspinall's Buildings.

Until late 1969 Aspinall's continued to trade at 89, Deansgate. The premises were taken over the following year by the Bolton Health Food Centre who, owing to successive building operations, had been compelled to move from nearby Old Hall Street North and later from Hotel Street.

From 1923 the Aspin Hall was one of Bolton's foremost dance halls – a place where the night could be danced away to the strains and beat of the Aspin Orchestra under the conductors' batons of trumpeter and cornetist Len Harlow and, for many years, pianist Joe Marshall. Joe played at the Aspin on its opening

and for a total of 22 years until his retirement in 1953. In 1965 the Hall became the Aspin nightclub but this closed in 1974.

Early in its life the Aspin had religious connections. In 1915-16, due to a most unfortunate rift between the Vicar of St Paul's, Deansgate, the Rev W Walker, and the congregation, the majority of the latter left the church and established themselves first in a building in Kensington Place and then in the Aspin Hall. An unusual situation arose. Whilst the major portion of his congregation held their Sunday services in the Hall, the vicar and a few of his supporters held theirs in the Church. This sad chapter in the church's history was closed when the Rev Walker left and the Rev J H Jones arrived. For years before 1924 the First Church of Christ Scientist held its meetings in the Aspin. In that year the congregation moved to new premises in Bromwich Street. Last year Whitaker's acquired Aspinall's Buildings, including the Aspin Hall, on a long lease.

Whitakers

The firm of Whitakers began in Bolton in 1870 when Yorkshire-born

John Whitaker and James Cain moved from Tyldesley to 22 Deansgate, and traded as Cain and Whitaker, drapers. The shop was situated across Wood's Court from the Bank of Bolton and was subsequently demolished for extensions to the Bank.

In 1874 Mr Whitaker bought out Mr Cain and the business became John Whitaker. Not long afterwards notice was given to quit and John Whitaker removed to 34 Deansgate, near the corner with Bridge Street. Widening of the latter in 1900 necessitated another move, this time to Yorkshire House, 99 Deansgate, a huge barn-like structure at the corner of Howell Croft North. This had a relatively short life in Whitaker's hands and the firm found its final resting place in a newly-built, half-timbered, Tudor-style building at 79-87 Deansgate. This was opened on November 7th, 1907, by the Mayor and Mayoress of Bolton, Alderman and Mrs Tong. Actually it was not open on the first day for the sale of goods, only for the public to look around. Also, for the first three days people were given free teas in the cafe.

At the time of this building's construction that part of the town centre was notorious and even policemen patrolled in twos. Practically everyone thought that the new store had been built in the wrong place. Everyone, that is, except John Whitaker junior, who had by then taken over from his father.

Over 70 years later, during which time the Oxford Street premises and others have been acquired and extensions and considerable internal alterations made, today's departmental store has certainly repaid the faith of its founder.

Old Hall Street

Before 1866, the year in which work began on the Town Hall, Old Hall Street ran from Deansgate through to Ashburner Street. The Old Hall from which the street took its name was Bolton's first house for the poor and from 1812 until 1820 the headquarters of the "Vigilance Association" for Great Bolton, who kept "watch and warrant" in the town. Granted a licence as the Three Arrows Inn in 1820, the building was subsequently demolished for corporation improvements after its licence had been transferred to the Park Inn, Bridgeman Street. The street was renumbered and renamed Old Hall Street North and Old Hall Street South in 1876.

No mention of the present-day Old Hall Street North can be made without referring to an establishment which in its 12 years in the street became an institution. The Casa Blanca coffee bar, opened in 1956, moved to Back Cheapside in 1968 and finally closed in 1971. It became well-known in Bolton and far beyond its boundaries for its coffee and home-made brown scones.

Oxford Street

Why Oxford Street was so called remains a mystery. One suggestion is that it is linked with the Civil War. Oxford was the starting point from which Prince Rupert marched North in May, 1644, and subsequently attacked and took Bolton in the third assault on the town. However, this is a very tenuous and most unlikely connection. Perhaps there was once a ford hereabouts which the oxen and ox-carts used to cross. On the other hand, maybe it was adopted simply because it was a good sounding title?

Over the years Oxford Street, albeit a shopping area in its own right, has also been the short link between Bolton's main square and Deansgate. Today it still serves that purpose, even more so since it became officially part of the Town Centre Precinct in 1973.

In the early 1920s the Bolton Co-operative Society purchased 1-15 Oxford Street. At that time these premises were owned by Ernest Barnes, tailor; Haddock's, milliners; James Monaghan, tailor and furrier; the Oxford Restaurant; Winward's,

tobacco and cigar dealers; and the St George and Dragon public house. Ernest Barnes moved to Chancery Lane and Monaghan's to Bradshawgate. The Oxford Restaurant, opened in the 19th century as the Oxford Coffee Tavern, closed down in 1924, the same year as the St George and Dragon public house. Winward's moved to Mealhouse Lane, where the firm ended its days in 1949 after 126 years of trading in the town.

Between the Co-op store and the Deansgate corner were Messrs Woolworth's, Riley's Temperance Billiard Hall which had earlier been in the Imperial Buildings, Deansgate, and the adjoining bank building which also housed Kay and Foley, photographers, and Bolton Wanderers Football and Athletic Company's office under the direction of Mr C E Foweraker, its long serving secretary/manager. Woolworth's subsequently gave way to Whitakers in 1926 and the photographer's and bank are still there. After 25 years above the bank, Bolton W.R.V.S. moved to new headquarters in St George's Road in 1980.

On the opposite side of the road were Holden's, wines and spirits; Fisher Raworth & Co. Ltd., ironmongers; Wilfred Johnson, hosier, glover, etc.; Fred Horsfall, tailor; Bradleys Ltd., clothiers and outfitters, and the Commercial Hotel. Not one of these businesses trades in the street today. On the closure of the Higher Nag's Head Hotel in 1929, Holden's moved for a time to St George's Road. Fisher

Oxford Street in 1907. The tall building housing Parr's Bank is still there. The remainder of the property was demolished to make way for the huge Co-op store and subsequently Whitaker's store.

Raworth, now in Spa Road, ceased trading at their Oxford Street premises in June, 1960; Wilfred Johnson closed in 1961 and Fred Horsfall ceased trading in 1955 after 40 years in the street. Bradleys have long since departed and the 18th century Commercial Hotel, which dominated the Victoria Square corner, closed in April, 1972, and was demolished later that year. Mothercare opened on its site in August, 1974.

Prominent in the centre of the precinct area at its Deansgate end is a piece, all 25 tons of it, of Bolton's industrial heritage. The mill steam engine was manufactured in 1886 by the Bolton firm of Hick, Hargreaves and Co., rescued from a silk mill at Low Bentham near Lancaster, and presented to the town by the firm.

Victoria Square

Victoria Square, today simply referred to as the Precinct, has maintained considerable links with Deansgate, particularly through its four short connecting streets. Looking at today's mass of concrete comprising the walking area and

shop fronts, it is hard to believe that about 170 years ago this area of Bolton had a delightful rural setting. An orchard, a meadow, even a bowling green, were the focal points of the area. Alongside the bowling green an idyllic little stream meandered its way southwards.

Progress was just around the corner, however, and in the 1820s, in order to avoid confusion and congestion brought about by market stalls which cluttered up parts of Churchgate, Deansgate and overflowed into adjoining streets, the New Market Place succeeded the basic rurality. At the opening of the New Market Square Mr Benjamin Hick presented a gas lamp which occupied a commanding position in its centre. Later his son presented a circular trough around its base, and a people's drinking fountain was also erected by public subscription. In 1925 trough and lamp were removed because their very presence would have distracted from the effectiveness of the projected War Memorial and they were also considered a menace to traffic. Both were transferred to the Mayor Street Depot, from where they were fin-

ally sold as scrap. The drinking fountain was removed to Queen's Park, where it still stands.

Overlooking the conglomeration of stalls were two imposing buildings, the 18th century Commercial Hotel and the Exchange Building at the Newport Street corner. The latter was erected in the 1820s as a newsroom for subscribers and a type of club. Later a library for members was opened upstairs. Subsequently, the building housed Public Library departments from 1853 until 1938 and today is principally occupied by the Nationwide Building Society.

Another eminent building for many years has been the solid stone edifice at the south-west corner of the Square. This was opened as a Lending Library in 1893 and remained as such until the new Public Library in the Crescent was ready for occupation in 1938. In 1948 the building opened its doors as the Victoria (Civic) Restaurant but this closed in 1951. Since then the building has housed National Insurance and local government offices before going full circle with the opening of the Bibliographic Serv-

The north side of Victoria Square in 1897. The ornate gas lamp and the circular trough surrounding its base were removed in 1925 because their presence would have detracted from the effectiveness of the War Memorial's setting and they were considered a menace to traffic.

ices Unit of the Bolton Public Libraries Department several years ago.

On the opening of the Market Hall in 1855 many of the stalls which occupied the Square and surrounding streets were moved into that building, whilst the remainder were later housed in the new wholesale market which opened behind the west side of Newport Street in 1871. With the opening of the Town Hall in 1873 and the fact that open-air trading no longer took place in the Square, a new name was deemed necessary for the area, and in June, 1873, it was renamed Town Hall Square. To commemorate the Diamond Jubilee of Queen Victoria, it became Victoria Square.

The impressive Town Hall was opened by the Prince of Wales on June 5th, 1873, and a considerable extension was virtually completed with the opening of the new Council Chamber in April, 1937. The opening paragraph in that part of the 72-page "Opening of Bolton Town Hall 1873" entitled "Architectural Description of the Town Hall" provides interesting, amusing and somewhat confusing reading – "The style of the building is a variety of that commonly termed 'Classic', and in regard to its general treatment may be most fitly described as 'Roman', though the details in it partake more of a Greek character, on the one hand, while the tower, on the other hand, belongs in general character to that modernised classic of the Renaissance period, which, as its revival took place originally in

The fleet's in. A collection of buses waits on Victoria Square in November, 1930, to take passengers to places as far afield as Bury, Heywood, Rochdale, Belmont, Harwood and Walshaw. From December 7th of that year a scene like this was no longer possible, for on that day buses ceased to use the Square as the town centre terminal and on the following day began to operate from alongside a temporary platform on Moor Lane parking ground. Note the War Memorial without its symbolic statuary. This was not added until 1932. The shops fronting the south side of the Square comprised the Singer Sewing Machine Co., which was entered from Newport Street, the Manchester Furnishing Warehouse, the Borough Engineer's Dept., Wood & Co., tea and coffee merchants, a forerunner of today's Health Food Centre, and on the corner of Old Hall Street South the Lancashire Wallpaper Co. On the opposite corner of Old Hall Street can be seen the Town Hall Hotel. The building was demolished in 1947.

Italy, has received the name of 'Italian'."

The total height of the front to the top of the balustrade is 63ft., the great hall rose out of the centre to a height of 81ft., the 10ft. square ventilating turrets rise 22ft. above this and the main tower to a total height of 200ft. In com-

parison, Blackpool Tower rises to a total height of 518ft. 9ins. Centrepiece of the imposing Victorian building, the Albert Hall, was wrecked by fire on November 14th, 1981.

Following the complete removal of market stalls from the Square came a long association with travelling fairs and menageries. Famous names like Sedgewick's, Mander's, Marsden's, Sanders', Edmunds', Wombwell's, Collins' and Parker's were regular attractions and over the years countless other names appeared on booths and roundabouts. During this time the small permanent fairground colloquially known as "Little Hell" moved from the Deansgate/Bridge Street corner to premises on the South side of the Town Hall and later to the Old Hall Street North corner. The proprietor was a Mr Forshaw, a relative of a family well-known in the fairground business, and the fair's attractions included a boxing booth, stalls, and goalkeepers who offered to stop the shots of people who fancied themselves as footballers. The great Joe Smith, Bolton Wanderers' captain and inside left, often went down on Friday evenings and what a treat he used to give the assembled crowd as

A modern bridge has replaced the old structure over Exchange Street and a television rental shop and a Wimpy Bar now stand where the front of the the Grapes Hotel was.

his left foot shots constantly rocketed into the net! "Little Hell" disbanded about 1922 and its site developed into a motley collection of wooden huts and hoardings. A booking office for his transport services was opened there by Mr J R Tognarelli. After the First World War Mr Tognarelli was one of the first people in Bolton to appreciate the possibilities of private road passenger services and long before his buses opened up regular services his chara-bancs were becoming a recognised holiday feature in the town. He had already created a carrying business of considerable size.

In February, 1927, Tognarelli and Co. began a through bus service to Manchester. This was extended in July, 1928, to Denton and Hyde. More than 12 months later, in December, 1929, the Tognarelli fleet of 26 buses was taken over jointly by the transport authorities of Bolton, Manchester, Salford, Oldham and L.U.T. Within the next two years two other private ventures were purchased; Messrs Orr's Motor Services Ltd. of Little Lever jointly by Bolton, Salford and Bury and "The Rocket" service which operated from Tonge Moor to Affetside, to Harwood and Brookfold Lane by Bolton Corporation.

"Togs" booking office subsequently became Arthur Christy's motor coach office, which later moved to Moor Lane. In 1948 the area was finally cleared and replaced by lawn and flower beds and in 1968 the adjoining property consisting of Betty's sweet shop and cafe; Hughes and Co., drapers and household goods; H Lee, grocer; Civil Defence Headquarters; the Health Food Store and La Casa Blanca coffee bar was demolished. On its site rose Victoria House which, in April, 1976, as part of the twinning ceremony with the German town of Paderborn, was renamed Paderborn House.

The statues of two prominent Boltonians have occupied positions flanking the Town Hall, one for over 100 years and the other for over 80 years. That of Dr Chadwick, prominent benefactor, was unveiled in August, 1873, and that of Sir Benjamin Dobson, local industrialist and Mayor of Bolton 1894-8, in February, 1900.

After the levelling of the Bessemer site at Moor Lane in 1927, the opportunity was taken to remove two features from the Square. The well-known New Year Fair ended its long-standing association in 1929 and began a 38 years' association with a site alongside Moor Lane. In December, 1930, Victoria Square ended its life as the town centre terminal point for buses and these began to operate from a temporary platform at the southern end of the Moor Lane parking ground.

Bolton Co-operative Society opened large premises at the corner with Oxford Street in July, 1928, and in the same month and year the War Memorial was unveiled by the Earl of Derby. In November, 1932, the two existing groups of statuary were placed in position on the memorial and unveiled. Sculptured by Walter Marsden, M.C., the group on the north side symbolizes "Struggle". The figure of "Peace" holds "Youth", characteristic of the best manhood of our town – clean and fit, with unbounded energy – prepared to give all for the country. The group on the south side typifies "Sacrifice", "Giving unto Death". Again there is the figure of "Peace" but this time she bears across her knees the prostrate body of "Youth" who has given himself to suffering and the agonies of death so that his country's honour may be preserved.

Major changes in the Square have taken place since the late 50s. At the same time that property was be-

A section of Victoria Square in September, 1954, just under 15 years before it became a traffic-free precinct. From the left and just out of sight is Naisby's store at the corner of Hotel Street followed by Northern House, ladies' fashions; Thomas Cook and Son, travel agents; Duckworth's, lingerie; Ye Olde Toffee Shoppe; Ribble Motor Services Ltd; Alstons, quality grocers; Bradshaws, pet food and accessories; Lumb and Smith, window furnishing specialists; T A Hindle, hardware and smallware dealer, and the Famous Army Stores. Just off the picture on the right is Hunter's dyers and cleaners and another Famous Army Stores. Between 1961, when Timothy Whites and Taylor's new premises replaced Naisby's, and November, 1969, when W H Smith & Son opened their new premises on the site of Northern House, the whole of this frontage was rebuilt.

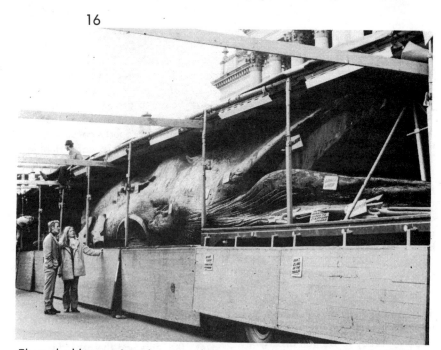

There she blows – since it was made into a precinct Victoria Square has been the scene of many exhibitions, stunts, concerts and the like. One of the most unusual exhibitions was that of a 66ft, 58-ton whale in April, 1970.

ing demolished on the west side of Newport Street in 1957, several shops on the south side of Victoria Square were also knocked down. One of these was the Singer Sewing Machine Co., which was transferred to the Deansgate end of Bradshawgate, subsequently into the Arndale Centre and then to Great Moor Street, its present location. The Manchester Furnishing Warehouse moved to the corner of Deansgate and King Street. Battersby's obtained temporary premises in the former Canon Slade Grammar School building before the firm moved in 1958 into newly-built premises on the east side of Newport Street, where it ended its Bolton days in 1973. Wood and Co. (Bolton) Ltd., tea and coffee merchants, ended a 126-years-old link with the Square when, in 1957, they moved to premises in Fold Street. The business finally closed in 1968 to make way for the Arndale Centre. The Health Food Store next door initially moved into Old Hall Street North, then Hotel Street and now trades in Deansgate. Finally, the Lancashire Wallpaper Co. moved to the corner of Deansgate and Central Street into premises now occupied by Hitchens. Property on the west side of Old Hall Street South was demolished in the late 1940s and included the former Town Hall Hotel at the corner with Victoria Square.

A building planned to conform with the Town Hall architecture was constructed on the Newport Street-Old Hall Street South side of the Square in 1960. Part was initially occupied by a self-service grocery store and is now Halford's motor car and cycle accessories shop; the remaining portion, occupied by the N.W.G.B. showroom and offices, opened in 1961.

Complete redevelopment of the block facing the Town Hall began in 1959-60. The Grapes Hotel and an old bridge over Exchange Street were demolished, and in March, 1961, Timothy Whites and Taylors, chemist (now Boots, chemist) moved into new premises on the site of the long-established Naisby's store at the Hotel Street corner. Messrs Naisby & Co. was founded in 1800 by William Naisby and moved to the Hotel Street site nearly 40 years later. The firm extended its business to include all kinds of drapery and soft furnishings and in its day the store was a fine example of the old-fashioned, large-size town drapers. A change of ownership occurred

early in 1955, the new owners being George Lavey & Co. Ltd. In November, 1958, Bolton Planning and Estates Committee approved an application by this firm to rebuild their shop premises, and in February, 1959, a lengthy "Closing Down Sale" began. Later it was announced that when it had been completed the building would be taken over by Timothy Whites and Taylor.

In 1963 the late Mr J W Wigglesworth, a Freeman of Bolton, offered to pay for an improvement scheme for Victoria Square involving tree planting, the erection of two fountains and permanent floodlighting for the whole of the Civic Centre. Plans were drawn up by the Borough Architect, Mr Geoffrey Brooks, and his staff and the scheme was completed in November, 1964.

On Monday morning, March 31st, 1969, all traffic was diverted from Oxford Street/Victoria Square/Newport Street North and Bolton's first pedestrian precinct swung smoothly into operation.

Subsequently flagged and landscaped, the precinct was officially opened in June, 1973, and since then has won three awards. The first, a Civic Trust European Architectural Heritage Year Award in 1975. The second, in 1977, the Concrete Society's Silver Jubilee Award for the best concrete landscape in the country, described as a "bold, well thought out and well executed scheme". In their report the judges said: "The use of concrete

as a surfacing material reflects the dignity of the civic architecture and provides a suitable urban floorscape". Finally, in April, 1978, the Manchester Society of Architects presented an award for initiative and enterprise in architecture.

The broad sweep of The Crescent at the rear of the Town Hall was renamed Le Mans Crescent in March, 1974, in honour of Bolton's first "twin" town, Le Mans, France.

It is not generally known or appreciated that overlooking the Square is statuary depicting Bolton's prominence in the industrial and commercial field. The tympanum of the pediment over the front of the Town Hall contains sculptured figures designed by the eminent sculptor, W Calder Marshall. He can best furnish a description of them:-

"The central figure represents Bolton, with a mural crown, and holding a shield on which is emblazoned the borough arms. The figures to the right and left (of the principal figure) represent 'Manufacturers' and 'Commerce'; the former holds a distaff and leans upon a bale of goods, whilst near her are a cylinder and wheel, symbolical of machinery; a negro boy bears a basket of cotton, and 'Earth' in the angle pours her gifts from a cornucopia. On the left of the principal figure is 'Commerce' holding the caduceus and a helm; a boy holds a boat by the bow, and in the angle is 'Ocean' typical of the extent over which the manufacturers of the town have spread. The figures are of Portland stone and upon a scale of eight feet if standing". The whole setting is today possibly more representative of the Borough than it was well over 100 years ago.

Hotel Street

Linking Mealhouse Lane with the precinct is Hotel Street, formerly Barrack Lane, a thoroughfare which since 1960 has been completely altered. Gone are the buildings which provided the street with its latest name, the Commercial Hotel (demolished 1972) and the Victoria Hotel. The latter closed in September, 1961, and was demolished along with the adjoining property including Stanley Haywood, chemist, and Naylors, tobacco and sweets, to make way for the third and final extension of Marks and Spencer Ltd.

Only the Bolton Trustee Savings Bank remains structurally unaltered. The Bank had its origin in 1818, when the Rev James Slade, Vicar of Bolton, opened the Bolton Bank for Savings in a small room in Oxford Street. Later a move was made to Wood Street, where the continual increase in business necessitated

another move to larger premises. Consequently, the present headquarters in Hotel Street, originally the old Bank of Bolton, was purchased and occupied in 1920.

Back Hotel Street has had close connections with the religious history of Bolton, as a plaque unveiled in 1949 on the side of the bank building recalls. The inscription reads- "On the right side of this street, then part of Acresfield, the first Methodist Chapel in Bolton in which John Wesley often preached was erected in 1751, and nearby, in the yard of the Old Nag's Head Inn, John Bennet conducted the first Methodist service in the town on Nov. 1st 1747. Erected by the Council of Methodist Circuits in Bolton." A blacksmith's shop which stood in Back Hotel Street until just over 30 years ago is said to have been part of the old chapel.

Opposite the bank the commanding Venetian-Gothic style gas office building stood for 95 years. Constructed in 1868 for the Bolton Gas Co., it passed into the hands of the State upon nationalisation in 1949. Closed in April, 1961, the building was taken over by a furniture, bedding and carpet firm before being demolished in 1963.

Today, the telephone is so much an accepted part of everyday life but over 100 years ago it was in its infancy or more specifically its babyhood. The first telephone experiment in Bolton actually took place on January 17th, 1878, from the Hotel Street gas offices and an article which appeared in the Bolton Weekly Journal of January 19th sets the scene:-

"A telephone, one of Pro. Bell's patents, had been attached to the telegraph apparatus in the Gas Offices and in the office at Gas Street ... and a number of gentlemen assembled in the Hotel Street office to test the capacity and power of the instrument."Conversations between the gentlemen and Mr Ahern, the telegraph contractor, were distinctly heard by the application of the tube to the listener's ear, as were musical items "Tommy make room for your Uncle" and "The Marseillaise" whistled at the Gas Street end. "Considerable satisfaction was expressed at the result of the experiments made."

British Home Stores now occupies the site of the building. Between the gas offices and Timothy White's premises a back street and the small but well-stocked wine and spirit shop of Ross, Munro and Co. Ltd. also disappeared in the 60s redevelopment.

At the bottom of the street George S Ikin Ltd., printers, moved out of their three-storey premises in 1960 into newly-built premises on Folds Road. Five years later the firm moved into part of the former Bradshaw bleachworks and, in 1971, closed its works at Bradshaw. C & A opened their premises on the Hotel Street/Chancery Lane site in November, 1970.

A shop at the corner of Acresfield, occupied for many years by the Central Fruit Stores and office property above, was demolished to make way for the Arndale shopping precinct, officially opened in September, 1971. The bridge across Hotel Street was constructed in 1966 to provide access for delivery vehicles.

As part of the Arndale development two prominent links with Hotel Street were severed, those of Chancery Lane and Acresfield.

Knowsley Street/Deansgate/ Oxford Street junction

Back to this junction which 50

A contrasting Hotel Street scene to the predominantly glass and concrete structures of today. Only the Bolton Savings Bank and the premises at the corner of Market Street remain from those shown in this 1950 photograph. Gone are the shops and offices at the corner of Acresfield, the gas offices, a wine and spirits shop, and Naisby's (top left). Shops and office property on the right and the Victoria Hotel were all demolished for construction of Marks & Spencer's store. The Victoria, whose host for many years was Frank Roberts, Bolton Wanderers, Manchester City, and England forward, was believed to have been the only hotel in Bolton to have enjoyed Royal patronage. In 1876, Prince Arthur, Duke of Connaught, was billeted there whilst accompanying a detachment of the 7th Hussars. From that time the hostelry sported over its doorway the Royal Coat of Arms.

years ago was the "Clapham Junction" of Bolton. Practically all trams trundled across it, whether heading into or out of the town and until 1928 a "points" boy was positioned here, whose job it was to dash into the middle of the roadway as a tram approached and with a pinch bar switch the points to the appropriate track. Considering the number of trams and other vehicles thereabouts, this was a somewhat dangerous practice and only a job for the extremely agile. Consequently, in 1928, a box containing "point" levers was installed on the pavement at the Knowsley Street corner on the east side of Deansgate. The points were made automatic in 1931-2. On the same corner until 1928 stood a rather dilapidated wooden structure, which served as the Corporation Tramways waiting room.

Major property changes in the late 20s and early 30s at the two easterly corners of the junction were initially brought about by a prominent present-day Deansgate firm, Whiteheads Ltd. During the rebuilding of their Deansgate premises in 1909, temporary premises were obtained at the corner of Deansgate and Oxford Street. Subsequently, when the new building was opened

it was felt that the Oxford Street corner offered too much potential to be given up and it was decided to continue trading there. A new company was formed under the title of T Bullough and Co. Ltd., the Paragon Dress House.

In the late 1920s Bolton Corporation wished to improve and widen the Oxford Street corner and, after lengthy negotiations, an exchange was made with Bulloughs – they were to have the opposite corner in place of the old tram shelter. Consequently, the building known as Knowsley House was constructed. Not only did it provide accommodation for the Paragon Dress House but also much-needed modern office and shop property. The whole building was completed in 1929.

The demolition of the former Paragon and adjoining property, George Winterburn, bookseller, and the Higher Nag's Head Hotel, also known as Holden's Vaults, took place in 1930. The Higher Nag's Head had been built in 1735 as the town residence of one John Andrews, who is also reputed to have built the beacon tower on Rivington Pike. An interesting aspect of the hostelry's demolition was the discovery of 45 coats of paint hiding the beauty

of the oak corbels on the door.

Weaver to Wearer, tailors, and Voses UCP Restaurant occupied newly-constructed property on the site of the public house and shop for many years (now Pizzaland Restaurant and Dixon Photographic respectively) and Brown Brothers and Taylor, furniture, subsequently moved into the new corner premises. Later, after the last named had established itself at the corner of Victoria Square and Exchange Street (premises now occupied by Woodhouses) Jackson the Tailors took over the shop in 1959 and remained there until 1978. Ratners, jewellers, are there today.

Palatine Buildings, diagonally opposite, is best remembered for its lengthy association with Burgons, Italian warehousemen and grocers, later Redheads, silk mercers and general drapers, and for many years up to 1981 the tailoring establishment of Alexandre.

At the turn of the century part of the site now occupied by the National Westminster Bank Ltd. was occupied by a public house called the Lion's Paw, previously known as the Four Horse Shoes. It was rebuilt in 1907 in pseudo-Tudor style,

From Knowsley Street looking along Oxford Street to Victoria Square over 50 years ago. Knowsley House had been completed in 1929 but the property on the opposite Oxford Street corner was awaiting demolition in 1930. Note the two 'boneshaker' trams, one open-ended top deck and the other enclosed top, also the 'cobbled' streets which preceded today's metalled roads.

changed its name to the Silver Vat two years later, and was demolished in 1927, when its licence was transferred to the Bowling Green, Bury Road. Parr's Bank, opened in Knowsley Street in the late 19th century, moved to the corner of Oxford Street in 1906. On the demolition of the Silver Vat, the bank was extended to occupy the whole of the Deansgate frontage between Oxford Street and Old Hall Street North.

Prominent at or near the Knowsley Street corner before Knowsley House days were Thomas Cook, travel agents (until the firm moved to Victoria Square), Gledsdale, printers, with their old-fashioned shop-fronted premises; Dodgson and Smith, costumiers and mantle makers, and Misses Charlton, ladies' and children's outfitters.

The Paragon Dress Shop on the Corporation Street corner eventually closed in 1965 and Derek Guest has been in the premises since 1970.

Knowsley Street

Before 1855 Knowsley Street was just a lane leading into a slum area. Consequent on the Bolton Improvement Act of 1850, it became a wide and handsome thoroughfare connecting Great and Little Bolton. The land on which the street was made belonged to the Earl of Derby but since a Derby Street already existed the new street was given the name of Knowsley, where the Earl's mansion was situated.

Many long-standing businesses have occupied sites in Knowsley Street this century. Amongst them was Horrocks Ltd. which was founded in Ridgway Gates in 1856 but had to wait until 1960 before having windows fronting on to the street. This was made possible when the firm acquired the Knowsley Street premises of Joan Barrie (Bolton) Ltd. Horrocks' closed in 1974 but reopened later in premises higher up the street. Joan Barrie subsequently moved into Oxford Street and in 1981 into Hotel Street.

Johnsons, dyers and cleaners, have carried on their trade for over 60 years, initially and for many years at 17 Knowsley Street, but more recently at No. 15. Previously 15-17 had been the offices of the Bolton Daily Chronicle, which began in 1824 and ceased publication in December, 1917.

Next door, J J Jones, costumiers and milliners, closed at the beginning of the 1970s, having traded

At first glance this building could quite easily be mistaken for the present pseudo Tudor-style building of Whitaker's. This is not surprising considering that it was constructed on the opposite corner of Old Hall Street North to Whitaker's in the same year, 1907, in which the latter opened. Obviously, the two buildings were erected in matching styles. The photograph actually shows the Silver Vat being demolished in 1927. Subsequently, Parr's Bank was extended to occupy the whole corner from Oxford Street to Old Hall Street.

there under that name since about 1909. Previously Messrs Ford and Cole, later just Benjamin Cole, had begun business there as silk merchants and general drapers in 1875. The building was demolished in 1973 and the new Co-op Bank opened on its site in September, 1975.

Golding, house furnishers, founded in 1850, joined with another old-established family furnishing business, Fryers, in 1957 and became Golding-Fryers and then simply Fryers. In February, 1982, Fryers announced the forthcoming closure of their stores. Haslam's, high-class grocers, closed as recently as 1976. Proffitts, radio and TV dealers, was founded in Knowsley Street in 1924. Later taken over by Lloyds, the premises today are occupied by

Horrocks'. Much earlier the well-known piano firm of Vickers had occupied part of the site. The firm advertised regularly at local cinemas, the main theme being a frock-coated pianist seated at a piano stool. As he began to play, the notes appeared by "magic" from under his frock coat.

The music shop and concert ticket booking agency of Thomas Coupe and Sons at 35 Knowsley Street closed its doors for the last time in 1959 and Edward Bullough Ltd, radio and TV dealer, extended their premises to take in the former shop. The concern became Rumbelow's in the 1970s.

Proprietors of a large store in Great Moor Street for over 60 years, Gregory and Porritt's opened the first phase of a three-storey showroom and office block in Bark Street in April, 1980. Incorporated in the new building was a shop already owned by the firm at the corner of Knowsley Street.

At the corner of St George's Road the St George's Hotel was demolished in 1972 and about that time all the old property on the east side of the street between the hotel and the Croal, including Morris's, photographers; Rothwell's, chemist; the Scotch Wool and Hosiery Store; Halford's, cycle dealers, and the N.W.E.B. showroom was demolished.

Opposite the hotel, the St George's Road Congregational Church opened as Bolton's leading Congregational Church in 1863. On amalgamation with the Presbyterian Church in 1972 it became St George's Road United Reformed Church and, in 1979, on its union with the now defunct St Andrew's

United Reformed Church, Bowker's Row, it took the grandiose title "The United Reformed Church of St Andrew and St George." A very prominent landmark in earlier days, it became less so in 1969 when its spire was removed as part of a massive renovation scheme.

The first Viscount Leverhulme was a prominent member of the church and "during his residence in Bolton he was regular at worship, constant in counsel, and his frequent appearances in the pulpit and on the platform left indelible impressions on the minds of those who heard him". In October, 1936, two beautiful stained glass windows given by his son in memory of his parents were dedicated at a special service.

Standing rather forlornly and overlooking Knowsley Street is the former St George's Church. One of the oldest churches in Bolton, it was built to seat 1,800 and consecrated in 1796 when there were less than 1,000

people in Little Bolton. The building was erected in a commanding position amidst pleasant surroundings on a hillside which sloped down to the River Croal. In order that the church could really be part of its surroundings, the builders were instructed to make the bricks on site from clay dug out of the hillside. The last service was held in July, 1975, and although many musical events have been held in the building since, its intended full use as a music centre is impossible at the present time owing to the economic situation.

Both McCartney's and "Pot" Bailey's have looked out from the Market Hall on to Knowsley Street since the 1890s and the Market Hall itself has provided much needed shopping space since it opened in 1855. Its main portico reflects classical traditions with an impressive Greek style facade of six elegant sandstone Corinthian columns supp-

A completely deserted Knowsley Street in 1902. Note the varieties of gas lamps and particularly the long stemmed one over the shop at the near right of the picture. The first Boots chemist's shop in Bolton is well advertised at No. 31 near the Victoria Hall. From Boots towards Palatine Street property included Mrs Redhead, draper (Redheads later opened in more extensive premises in Palatine Buildings at the Knowsley Street/Deansgate corner). Next came Golding and Son, later Fryers. Collinsons Orient Cafe ended its days in 1967. Adjoining the cafe, Richard Day was making and selling umbrellas and walking sticks. Benjamin Cole, near left, was subsequently taken over by J J Jones, a firm which closed down in the early 1970s. Dominating the skyline at the top of the street are the tower of St George's Church and the spire of St George's Road Congregational Church. The latter lost its spire in 1969 and the former is no longer a church.

orting a handsome pediment.

Opposite the Market Hall, the Victoria Hall has been the home of Methodism in Bolton since 1900. It also provides the town with a social and entertainment centre where many concerts and recitals are held.

Three other "social centres", only one of which, alas, is still in existence, are worth mentioning. Talbot's, Collinson's and Percival's cafes/restaurants over the years popularised Knowsley Street. Talbots, founded in Deansgate, spent its last years in Knowsley Street. When it closed in 1959, the building was incorporated into the premises of Messrs Proffitt's. Collinson's, on the street for 70 years, served its last "cuppa" in November, 1967. A victim of a change in eating habits, it had established itself in the period when lunch was the main meal of the day. Consequently, when many people became content with a quick snack at mid-day and ate their main meal at home in the evening, trade gradually fell and eventually it was no longer practicable to remain open. Percival's,

however, still has its clientele. Percival's Creamery provided teas and light refreshments for many years up to 1939, when the Clarke family concern took over. In 1971 the Lamplighter Restaurant was opened under shops fronting Knowsley Street.

Scholl's, footwear specialists, have occupied their premises in Knowsley House since the construction of the building 50 years ago.

Knowsley Street to Millwell Lane

Just over 50 years ago the shop at the present time sandwiched between John Collier and Samuel's was owned by Fifty Shilling Tailors. The firm later took over much larger premises in Knowsley House and for many years after their removal the small shop was owned by successive furriers, Dodgson's and Swears and Wells. In 1971 it opened as the Golden Egg Restaurant and recently as Bolton's second existing Wimpy Bar.

Samuel's

Samuel's, jewellers, who already

had premises alongside Millwell Lane, took over an adjoining shop in 1963. This, from 1915 until 1929, had been Marks and Spencer's first Deansgate premises. Complete rebuilding took place and the extended shop was opened by Samuel's in September 1963. In the meantime a continuous service had been maintained from a temporary shop in Victoria Square. Much earlier, for several years up to 1906, in fact, H Samuel, watchmaker and jeweller, had occupied premises at the corner of Bradshawgate and Fold Street.

Millwell Lane

Between Samuel's and the Co-op Pharmacy one of Bolton's narrowest lanes connects Deansgate and Corporation Street. The name Millwell when linked with those of Cockerell Springs, Spa Road, Silverwell Street, Spring Gardens, Halliwell (Holy Well) and Well Street, lends credence to the belief that centuries ago Bolton was famous for its many wells and springs.

It has been said that Millwell Lane was not always so called and was Silverwell Street long before

A conglomeration of produce and merchandise. The Market Hall in the early days of this century before the opening of the Ashburner Street Market in 1932 . In 1935 the Markets Committee, having realised that by modern standards the layout of the Market Hall and its organisation left much to be desired, approved a scheme for complete reorganisation and modernisation of the interior. Work began in August, 1935, and the "new" Market Hall with up-to-date layout incorporating blocks of stalls of modern design was officially opened in April, 1938. For many years before this modernisation the balcony around the inside of the building housed stalls exhibiting and selling domestic pets of all descriptions and a visit to it was a must for junior members of the family.

Marks and Spencer's Bazaar which occupied 60, Deansgate, from 1915–1929.

that name was transferred to the street off Bradshawgate. Certainly, and contrary to popular opinion, there is a strong possibility that the famous Silver Well of old was not in the vicinity of the present-day thoroughfare which bears that name but was found earlier this century under the shop occupied by Mr Wilfred Johnson (later Messrs Plumbs and now Waldmans) in Market Street. Whilst a cellar was being modernised, a well of remarkable depth was discovered with the name "Silver Well" set in quaint characters on a covering stone. Three lines of wooden pipes were also discovered running in different directions. There is no need for local traders to worry that their premises may one day be flooded by the well brimming over. It was lowered below cellar level and pipes laid from it into the Oxford Street sewer.

Incidentally, the finding of the well in Market Street does not take any of the glory from Silverwell Street. Several old wells have been

found in and about that area, any of which could have provided the street with its distinctive name.

At the Corporation Street corner with Millwell Lane Emily Kenyon opened a fashion store in 1928. In 1954, whilst adjoining property which had been taken over by the firm was being remodelled, there was a near disaster when the entire front section collapsed, burying and injuring two women. The new premises subsequently opened in November, 1954, and six years later E Kenyon Ltd. opened a new modernised showroom and also a new shop "The Gallery" in Millwell Lane.

Bolton's long-standing parking problem was ultimately blamed for the loss to the town of Kenyon's. A notice displayed in the shop window in 1978 announcing its closure read "moving to Horwich, where parking is easy."

Co-operative Society Pharmacy

The site of the Co-op Pharmacy

(now Harris Carpets on the Deansgate/Market Street corner) before the 1880s was occupied by Fernihough and Co., grocers and Italian warehousemen. The block, which included premises in Market Street, was reconstructed in 1880 and given the grandiose name "Financial Buildings". Fernihough's subsequently moved into premises between Constantine's and the Bank of Bolton, where they also opened the well-known Mimosa Cafe. This apparently served a dual purpose. In the morning and afternoon of weekdays it provided a pleasant cup of coffee or tea and a meeting place for the businessmen of the town, whilst in the evening it was a popular rendezvous for young people. For many years one of its rooms served as the headquarters of Bolton Chess Club and many of the world's greatest chess masters, including Capablanca, played there. The Mimosa also boasted a special ladies' room and a gents' smoke room. The cafe was later sold to Constantine Brothers and upon Woolworth's taking over the store they also took over the Mimosa and incorporated it into their premises.

Meanwhile, about 1886, a William Green, who had at one time worked for William Fernihough and later on his own at a shop in Corporation Street, moved into the former Fernihough's premises. He carried on business there for 34 years as grocer, Italian warehouseman and druggist, until the building was bought by Bolton Co-operative Society. The Society officially opened its new shop in September, 1921. This included departments for the sale and working of jewellery and also optical, drugs and photographic sections. In 1961 the premises were rebuilt and a new pharmacy opened for business in November of that year. This closed in 1981 on transfer of its business to the Oxford Street store and the premises are now used by Harris Carpets.

Market Street

Consequent on the opening of the New Market Place, a street joining it and Deansgate was appropriately named New Market Street. Later, the appellation "New" was dropped and, with the building of the Market Hall, the street was continued across Deansgate and down Taylor Brow to the side of the Hall building.

The oldest firm still in existence with Market Street connections, although it is not now in the town centre, is Robert Kenyon Ltd. Begun in Oxford Street in 1848, it moved to Market Street the following year. The printing department moved to premises in Liptrot Street in 1946, as did the bookbinding department from Blackhorse Street. Finally, all connection with Market Street was severed in 1965 when, after 117 years, the stationery department was moved to Lark Hill, St George's Road. Kenyon's, now an Associated Company of Blackshaw, Sykes and Morris Ltd., made their last move in 1973 to the former St Mark's Church of England Day School, Fletcher Street, a building over 100 years old.

Speaking of Kenyon's brings to mind the fact that Market Street was, in its early years, a minor "Fleet Street". Robert Kenyon printed the Bolton Temperance Messenger there about 1849 and this continued as a monthly magazine and representative organ of the Young Men's Temperance Society for many years. It was very popular and had a wide circulation in Sunday Schools.

Further, at No. 7, the premises taken over by Robert Kenyon, the Bolton Free Press (1835-47) began its early life under John Ogle, as did the very short-lived Bolton Reflector, a "Weekly Miscellany of Literature, Criticism, the Arts and Sciences, Biography, Topography, Poetry and Anecdotes". A grandiose name, but one which the journal obviously did not live up to, for it ceased publication in 1823 after only 19 numbers had appeared. According to Barton in his "Historical Gleanings of Bolton and District" it would better have been described as a "Weakly Miscellany..."

Brown's Trimming Shop, the shop with the "old fashioned atmosphere", moved to Bridge Street in March, 1976, after 94 years in Market Street.

Very few town centre premises have remained substantially unaltered since the middle of the 19th century. Blain's chemist's shop, established in 1851 and now trading under the heading of Hart's Chemist, is one of them. Behind the hand-made brick facade, most of the interior is original Victoriana. Fittings for riot screens are still in existence and the latter could be moved across the windows from inside the shop in an emergency.

Other long-standing businesses which disappeared after the War but of which memories linger on are Sugden's, with its reputation of being the leading baby-linen shop in Lancashire devoted exclusively to that purpose; Seed's grocery; Seddon's Cosy Cafe; Tyler's, boot and shoe manufacturers; Wilson's, costumiers; and Beaty Brothers, who could measure you for a suit and deliver it the next day. Wilfred Johnson erected fine premises (from 1972 until 1981 occupied by Plumbs and since Waldmans) in the 1920s and continued trading there for nearly 40 years. Before being taken over by Telehire in 1959, the Engineering Service Co., electrical engineers and contractors, vied with the now defunct Pearl Radio for the sale of the gramophone records of the day.

In the 1870s the Union Bank of Manchester opened a branch in Deansgate but this was relatively shortlived and we soon find them at 1, Bradshawgate. In 1901 a move was made to the present site at the Market Street/Deansgate corner. Today's impressive building, under the name of Barclay's Bank, opened in April, 1961.

At the other end of the street the Maypole Dairy Co. came in about 1910 and represented one of the first of the multiple store invaders. Opposite, the 82-years-old drapery business of F Steel and Son was taken over in 1955 by Bolton Co-operative Society, who opened it as a tailoring department the following year. Through this purchase the Society acquired all that block of property. The tailoring department was transferred to the Oxford Street premises in 1981 and the building was then taken over by the Beauty Care Drug Store.

Market Street is still a popular shopping area but at the same time it has branched out into the realms of entertainment with the opening many years ago of the Mill Hill Bingo and Social Club and more recently Cascade, Bolton town centre's first bingo and amusement centre.

Williams & Glyn's Bank

The imposing edifice which houses Williams and Glyn's Bank on the corner of Market Street had its origins in 1818 in Water Street when, in what later became the Grapes Hotel, a quintet of businessmen began a banking venture. Upon a later move to the Market Street/Corporation Street corner the business became known as Hardcastle, Cross and Co. A prosperous business expands and consequently, in August, 1875, the bank moved to the spacious premises which it occupies today.

In 1890 it became Williams Deacons and Manchester and Salford

A bustling Market Street scene despite the rain in March, 1948. From the Commercial Hotel, part of which appears on the left of the photograph, premises included Kenyon's, stationers; Sugden's, baby linen; Wilfred Johnson, draper; Tyler's, shoe retailers; Blain's, chemist, and, on the corner with Deansgate, the former Barclays' Bank building. Wilson's occupied the Hotel Street corner for many years. Subsequently, the premises housed Van Allen until July, 1981, and from the end of that year Timpson's shoes. Two wedding cars wait patiently for guests, who are obviously partaking of a meal at Seddon's Cosy Cafe.

Bank Ltd. but 11 years later this un-wieldy title became simply Williams Deacons Bank Ltd. Extensions in 1925, an amalgamation with Glyn, Mills and Co. in 1970 which resulted in a change of title to Williams and Glyn's Bank Ltd., and major internal alterations completed in 1979 have combined to provide the town with a bank of "the time" and one of Will-iams' largest branches in the country.

Burton's and Tognarelli's

Burton's bought out the large and old established firm of Shaw, Stur-gess and Co. in the 1920s and re-modelled the premises in 1940. Twelve months before this purchase the firm had acquired the Peake's Place Mill, Halliwell, of Walter Mather and Co. Ltd. and opened what was then claimed to be the sixth largest clothing factory in Europe. This closed down at the end of 1978.

Over Burton's was the well-known Savoy Cafe of Tognarelli's and, in the same building for several years, one of Bolton's many billiard halls of that era, the King's Billiard Hall.

The name of Tognarelli became a household word not only in Bolton but throughout South Lancashire gen-erally. A doyen of the ice-cream and cafeteria business, Mr John Robert Tognarelli also opened long-distance road haulage, coach serv-ices, and a pioneering bus service during his 63 years of working life in England. He opened his Market Street cafe and ice-cream parlour in the late 1920s and memories are recalled of "Owd Tog" wearing his characteristic white apron ruling both staff and customers with a rod of iron. He retired from business in 1960 and died four years later.

Lower Nag's Head Hotel

The Lower Nag's Head Hotel dates back centuries. However, the growing importance of Deansgate as a business centre, coupled with the increase in road traffic, required road widening earlier this century and involved the disappearance of many of the old picturesque buildings characteristic of an earlier age. One such was the Lower Nag's Head which, in 1927, was pulled down and replaced by an imposing three-storey structure. This was opened on December 8th of that year. In 1967 it really became the "Lower" Nag's Head when the two bars at ground floor level were closed. To counteract this loss, the downstairs lounge was extended by the addition

of a former substantial cellar. After considerable alterations, the former ground floor was opened in May, 1967, to house Hepworth's, multiple tailors.

Dunn and Co., at the corner of Mealhouse Lane for nearly 40 years, was the last shop to be demolished for extensions to Marks and Spencer. It was later opened in part of the old Marks and Spencer building in 1967, to allow the whole of the present Deansgate frontage to be completed.

Marks & Spencer's

Marks and Spencer opened their Penny Bazaar in the Market Hall in the 1890s and on their first Saturday afternoon of business they took £20 in pennies. A considerable amount in that day and age.

A shop at 60, Deansgate, now swallowed up by extensions to Sam-uel's, jewellers, was acquired in 1915 and closed in 1929 with the opening of a new and larger shop on the other side of Deansgate. Part of this building's upper exterior can still be seen over Dunn and Co's shop.

The construction of the present substantial premises began in 1965 and had meant earlier demolition of not only the Bay Horse Hotel ("Scotch Vaults") but also all the property on the west side of Meal-house Lane. Consequently premises of established businesses like H S

Taylor (jewellers), Makinson (fancy goods), Kavanagh's (tailors), Stan-ley Haywood (chemist), Ransome & Co. (oyster bar) disappeared, along with several Hotel Street premises.

The old store in Deansgate closed for business in April, 1967, on the completion of the first stage of Marks and Spencer's extension. The second section, opened in Novem-ber, 1967, and the one on Hotel Street, which marked the complet-ion of the building project, opened in June, 1968.

Williams & Glyn's Bank - Bridge Street

Two previous occupants of the shop which until recently housed New Day, furnishers, were Abraham Lincoln, household goods, and for several years up to the 1930s T Sey-mour Meade's, grocers, with its up-stairs cafe/restaurant. Here the pro-cess of eating and drinking and carrying on scintillating convers-ations was accompanied by the sound of music played by the regular ensemble.

The property adjoining, also own-ed by a furnishing store for many years, later a carpet showroom, was constructed in 1884, as its date stone confirms. Previously the site had been occupied by the Rose and Crown Inn, which was demolished in that year after its licence had been transferred to the Railway

The Marks and Spencer's store in Deansgate, which opened in 1929 and closed in 1967. Part of the old building can be seen today above Dunn & Co's tailoring establishment. On the left of the picture is the famous Talbot's Cafe shortly before it removed to Knowsley Street. On the right the frontage of the Lower Nag's Head Hotel.

Hotel, St Helens Road. The exterior of the upper floor remains as it was nearly 100 years ago, when the ironmongery business of George Graveson and Sons moved there from premises higher up the "Gate". The firm moved out about 50 years later.

Incidentally, Fisher Raworth and Co. Ltd. took over the business of Gravesons in 1935 and consequently acquired their two shops, one in Bradshawgate and the other in Market Street, Farnworth.

Boots later appeared on the scene as owners, and here lies a strong connection with the property at the corner of Bridge Street. The site of this has had a most interesting history over the past 80 years. Part of it was occupied by the Rope and Anchor Inn, which closed in 1899 as a result of the transfer of its licence to the Halliwell Lodge Hotel. Next to the Rope and Anchor, a silk mercer and family draper, William J Stocker, was occupying the premises when Deansgate was rapidly growing in commercial value in the 1870s. Subsequently, John Whitaker, founder of the firm we know today as Whitakers (Bolton) Ltd., acquired the site. In 1900 the Corporation decided to widen the entrance to Bridge Street and gave Mr Whitaker notice to quit.   He was loth to leave the shop, and the Corporation had to pull down the premises on either side of him and even started the assault on his own premises before he moved to 99 Deansgate.

After completion of the street improvements, the site remained empty for several years and during this time had an association with a motley collection of fairground booths, fortune-tellers and goalkeepers who offered to stop the shots of people who fancied themselves as footballers. This permanent fairground was known as "Little Hell".

On the construction of the Electric Theatre, "Little Hell" moved to the south of the Town Hall before ending its days on the site of what is now Paderborn House. The Electric Theatre, opened in 1910, was Bolton's first custom-built cinema. Later it took the title Imperial Playhouse before becoming the Embassy Cinema. Many people will still recall a film show, tea and biscuits, all for a "tanner". The cinema was eventually closed in 1947. Littlewoods Stores Ltd. reopened the building the following year and traded there until 1957, after which date Boots appeared, or rather reappeared, for they were already sited next door.

Boots actually opened in Bolton at the turn of the century at 31, Knowsley Street, and by the time the 1907 Bolton Directory had been published the firm had also taken over the adjoining building. For many years the business remained in Knowsley Street until the acquisition of premises next door but one to the cinema in Deansgate. In 1958 the firm purchased the former Littlewood's building and adjoining property and, after demolition, built their present extensive store, which was opened in October, 1961. Boots' building on Victoria Square was opened by Timothy Whites in March, 1961, and taken over by the present firm some years later.

Cinema closures

It now seems incredible that in the late 1930s the Embassy, or the Imperial as it was known then, was one of 22 cinemas open at the same time in Bolton. Today there are only three, one of which caters solely for the Asian community in the town.

Of the 22, the Hippodrome was the first to cease showing films in 1940, followed seven years later by the Embassy. The decline really set in in the 50s with the closure of the Astor (originally Olympia and later Regal), Spa Road in 1955; Empire,

Recognise anybody? A crowded Deansgate scene in 1949. Abraham Lincoln's has today given way to New Day, furnishers (closed March 1982) and Boots to Allied Carpets (closed March 1982). Littlewoods had moved into the former Embassy Cinema and remained there until 1957. Along with the adjoining small shop the premises were demolished and the site is now occupied by Boots' extensive store, opened in 1961. Woolworth's was extended and reconstructed in 1957-9

Howard Street, 1956; Palace, Bury Road, 1956; Belle, Astley Bridge, 1957; Palladium, Higher Bridge Street, 1957; Majestic, formerly Rumworth, St Helens Road, 1958; Gem, Shepherd Cross Street, 1958; Crompton, Crompton Way, 1959; Ritz, formerly Atlas, Fletcher Street, 1960; Carlton, formerly Mount, Mount Street, 1960; Rialto, St George's Road, and Tivoli, Derby Street, 1960; Windsor, formerly Plaza, Deane Road, 1962; Theatre Royal, Churchgate, 1962; Regent, Deane Road, 1967; ABC, formerly Capitol, Churchgate, 1977. The Royal, St George's Road, showed its last English film in 1967. The Queen's Cinema, built in 1912, showed its last English film in 1970 and from that year until its closure in 1980 it catered for the Asian community in Bolton.

Cinemas which did not run concurrently with the 22 of the 1930s were the Ideal, Silverwell Lane, 1907-16 and the Beehive, Bark Street, closed in 1927. The Princess Cinema, Churchgate, was incorporated in the Theatre Royal extension in 1928; the Picturedrome ("T' Scope"), Tonge Moor Road, was destroyed by fire in 1930, whilst the Paragon, Bradshawgate, closed in 1930 and five years later was demolished to make way for a shopping arcade.

Of the three remaining cinemas in the town the Rialto re-opened as the Apollo Cinema in 1978. The Lido, opened in 1937, became Studio I & II in 1970 and the Odeon, also opened in 1937, became a triple cinema in 1972.

Bridge Street junction

Mention has been made of the large amount of traffic which at one time crossed the Deansgate/Oxford Street/Knowsley Street junction. This is certainly confirmed by statistics revealed during re-routing of trams in Bridge Street in the 1930s.

Up to May 27th, 1933, inward-bound Dunscar, Halliwell and Tonge Moor trams used to come up Bridge Street, turn right into Deansgate, along to Oxford Street and then left to Trinity Street. From May 28th, however, a few months after the demolition of the old Bridge Street Fish Market, these cars were re-routed along Corporation Street and Knowsley Street, and then straight through to Trinity Street. This re-routing meant an incredible total of 675 fewer trams per weekday (a

After reading all the adverts fronting the old Imperial Playhouse, Deansgate, in this 1920s picture, one is left with no doubts that the film about to be shown there was "The Mystery Man" starring "Gentleman" Jim Corbett, former World Heavyweight Champion. The man on the pavement was the manager of the cinema for nearly 20 years, Mr Walter Sutton. At that time Meesons, confectioners, on the Bridge Street corner also had a shop on the opposite side of Deansgate and two in Bradshawgate. Over the shop the huge advert for Lion Oils was Moscrop's symbol for many years. On the opposite side of Bridge Street, Woolworth's had obviously not taken over from Constantine's.

figure quoted at the time) travelling along the congested stretch of Deansgate from Bridge Street to Oxford Street.

The last service tram ran along Deansgate on October 6th, 1946, on which day the Horwich tramcar service was abandoned.

Trams - the beginning and end

Whilst on the subject of trams it is appropriate at this stage to recount the growth and decline of this form of transport in Bolton.

Horse trams ceased to operate in the town on January 2nd, 1900. Meanwhile, in December, 1899, electric tramcars commenced running on the Tonge Moor, Tootill Bridge and Great Lever routes. The following month other cars ran to Lostock, Doffcocker, Daubhill, Halliwell, Deane, Dunscar and Moses Gate, and between then and 1924 when the Westhoughton service began many additional routes were added. Bolton's first permanent bus service - Victoria Square to Lowther Street - began in December, 1923, and by the end of 1928 the number of bus services was in the teens.

Tram closures subsequently took place thick and fast. The major ones were Darcy Lever (A), which was replaced by motor buses on March 11th, 1928; Church Road (S), March 1, 1933; Bury (B), January 22, 1934; Hulton Lane (R), March 29, 1936; Great Lever (G), May 1, 1936; Swan Lane (M), popularly known as "Miffy" after an Evening News cartoon character, August 17, 1936; Dunscar (D), October 4, 1937; Montserrat (O), January 1, 1939; Halliwell (H), August 14, 1939 - but this later ran as a wartime measure; Walkden and Farnworth (Black Horse) (F), November 13, 1944; Horwich (N), October 7, 1946; Westhoughton (E), November 4, 1946; Deane (E), December 9, 1946. When the last service tram ran on the Tonge Moor route (T) on March 29, 1947, the abandonment of the tram service in Bolton was complete, the "rattle-traps" were to sway and judder along the tracks no more, and a colourful era in the town's history had ended.

Bridge Street

As its name suggests, Bridge Street passes over the River Croal, though the structure of the bridge itself has taken various forms over the years. In 1898 there was a proposal to change the name from Bridge Street to Blackburn Road throughout, but in view of the outcry from traders and others the Streets Committee left it to be known by the old name.

Today Bridge Street is widest at its lowest level but up to the 1930s this was its narrowest section. The cause, the old Fish Market, a building possessing a certain architectural charm, which stood alongside Rushton Street with its side facing the rear entrance to the Market Hall. When the Fish Market was demolished in 1932-3, following the opening of the new Ashburner Street market, this finally removed a bottleneck which had been in existence for 67 years.

An interesting event was witnessed early one morning, shortly before a start was made on the building's demolition. A huge army of rats was seen marching in formation up Bridge Street. Obviously a classic example of rats leaving a sinking ship. But who told them the ship was about to sink, and where were they heading?

At the corner of Lorne Street, Howard's tobacconist's shop has occupied the site for well over 100 years and is the oldest tobacconist's in Bolton. J F Turner (Tools and Cutlery) Ltd. moved from Deansgate, where Whitakers now stands, to 18, Bridge Street (premises now occupied by Carpets Galore) at the turn of the century and carried on trading there until March, 1962, when the stock was transferred to their stall in the Market Hall. Several years ago the firm was taken over "lock, stock and barrel" by Messrs Oxendales.

From the 19th century until 1957

Bolton Co-operative Society had carried on business in Bridge Street in a row of small, separate shops. In that year they were torn down and, in September, 1958, the present supermarket was opened on the site. Further along Bridge Street on the opposite side of the road stood one of the town's prominent landmarks, the Flax Mill chimney, owned for many years by William Holt Ltd., cotton spinners and doublers, of Bark Street. Town Planner Graeme Shankland campaigned in 1965 for its retention as a "symbol of a new Bolton" yet, at the same time, one which could be regarded with sentiment as a relic of another age. Unfortunately, his dream was not a practical proposition and in 1972 the chimney was demolished.

Nearby, John Prest, claimed to be the oldest established shoe shop

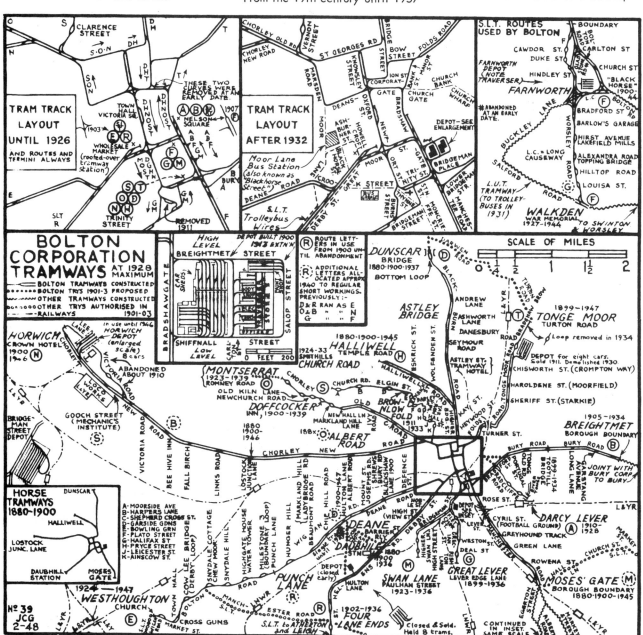

The growth of public transport in Bolton from the horse trams of 1880-1900 through electric traction 1899-1947 to motor buses 1923-48

in Bolton, started in premises on its present site in 1857. The shop is due for demolition in the not too distant future to make way for the multi-million pound Bark Street shopping complex. Across the road, Peerless Shoe repairs has fronted Bridge Street since 1923 and until July, 1980, when it changed hands, was under the control of the Roberts family, father and son. Crane's, leather goods dealer, established in 1907, is still at 44, Bridge Street. At the corner of Bow Street the New Market Inn was closed in December, 1973 and demolished the following January.

Memory lingers on of another long-standing family concern connected with the street. Bowe's Ltd., clothiers and drapers, more often referred to as "The shop with the Man at the Door" because of the life-size model positioned at the

entrance to the shop, originally opened in 1912 fronting the Fish Market. Around that time corduroy and moleskin trousers, ready or made to wear, could be obtained from the firm for 4s 11d (24½p), shirts for 1s 11d (9½p), socks for 6½d (2½p) and a "good black suit" for 11s 6d (57½p). A move was made to the Bark Street corner in 1928 and the Bowe family finally bowed out in 1979, upon closure of their last premises in Newport Street.

At the corner of St George's Road stands a building which has been associated with the entertainment life of Bolton for over 50 years. The Palais de Danse opened in October, 1928, and countless people, both young and old, have danced the light fantastic, and in many cases not so light, across its floor. Famous resident bands included those of Tommy Arnold,

and local legend Johnny Healey, followed by Jimmy Nowell and then Phil Foster. Mecca Dancing Ltd. took over in 1957 and introduced the Eddie Shaw Band, Peter Legh and his orchestra, Les Moss and his band, Phil Moss, the Ken Phillips Band and the Denis Langfield Sound. A fire in July, 1977, wrecked the building which, after renovations and remodelling, opened in May, 1979, as the nightspot, Rockerfellas (now Cinderellas Rockerfellas).

In close proximity to Rockerfellas stand two buildings whose architectural styles contrast strongly. The striking and imposing terra-cotta block which since 1976 has housed the Prescription Pricing Authority of the National Health Service was built in 1896 for the Co-op Drapery Department and opened the following January. At that time it was the

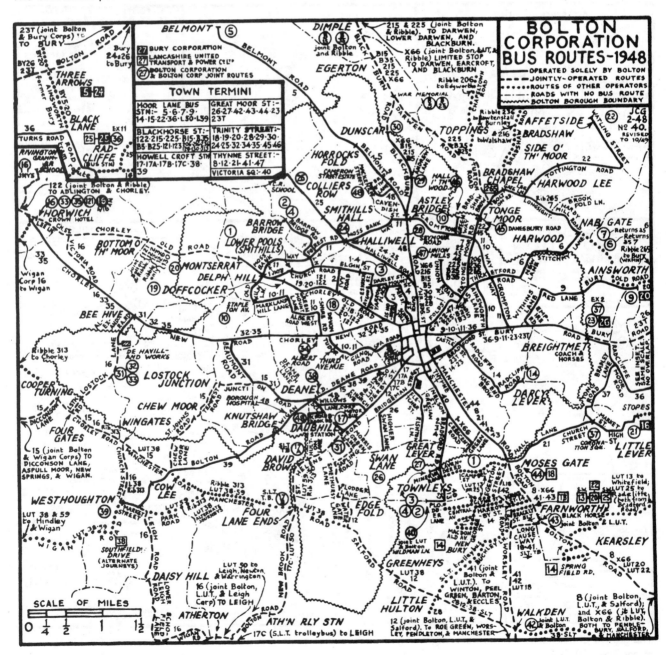

largest ever built in the town for a retail business. Practically destroyed by fire in 1902, it was rebuilt and in Co-op hands until 1952, when the N.W.E.B. took it over. The latter moved out to premises alongside Manchester Road in 1971.

Situated on the corner of Higher Bridge Street and St George's Street stands the attractive Georgian brick building, formerly Bridge Street Methodist Church. Opened in 1804 as the "New Chapel" to distinguish it from the Ridgway Gates "Old Building", it closed in 1969.

Museum of Local History and Moscrop's Lion Motor Oils

At the corner of All Saints Street and St George's Street, the former Little Bolton Town Hall opened as Bolton's first Museum of Local History in March, 1978. The building had served as a Town Hall, public meeting room and courtroom until the opening of the present magnificent town centre structure in 1873. Several years later it became a public library and ultimately a workshop. Today, highlights of events and living conditions over the centuries, coupled with frequent exhibitions, make the building and its contents valuable adjuncts to the

town's principal museum.

One of the first presentations to the new Museum was a larger than life John Bull figure standing in a barrel advertising Moscrop's Lion Motor Oils. Moscrop's was founded in 1838 in already existing stone-built premises on the opposite side of St George's Street. Taken over in 1972 by a Manchester-based oil firm, it was closed down in May, 1978, after 140 years of production.

Corporation Street

Corporation Street owes its origin to the construction of the Market Hall in 1855. The latter had swept away much slum property thereabouts and four new streets were, in effect, created - Knowsley Street, Brook Street, Rushton Street (named after Alderman Thomas Rushton, Mayor of Bolton during the inauguration of the Market Hall) and Corporation Street, which was so titled to commemorate this great civic achievement of the mid-19th century.

For the first 40 years of its life Corporation Street remained something of a nonentity with uninspiring shops on one side and a blank, prison-like wall on the other. However, in 1894, the wall was pierced and shops fronted the Market Hall building, giving a more balanced

look to the street. With the pulling down of the old Fish Market at its Bridge Street end, road widening thereabouts and re-directing of incoming trams along its short length, Corporation Street became a busier and a developing thoroughfare.

This is not to say that it had not been busy before 1933. It had, but at a different time of the day. Before the Shop Assistants Act became law, the Market Hall was open until 9.00pm on Mondays, 8.00pm Tuesdays, Wednesdays and Thursdays, 9.30pm on Fridays and 11.00pm on Saturdays, and before the advent of the cinema it was a meeting place both inside and out for the young people of the town. Until very late on a Saturday night, rival vendors in the Fish Market used to vie with each other in offering sixpence and shilling parcels of fish, or a rabbit with accessories, to belated shoppers.

Today, the two longest standing businesses in the street are McCartney's, which has been there since the turn of the century and Hartley's, which celebrated its Diamond Jubilee occupancy of the Market Hall in 1980. The staircase which connected the Market Hall shop with storerooms above became something of a hallmark for this firm and is remembered as a tribute to earlier craftsmen. It consisted of a spiral of 23 steps made entirely of wood and not attached to a central pillar. No nails were used in its construction, the whole being dovetailed and jointed together. Unfortunately it had to come down in 1970 but a small section was kept intact and preserved in the joinery department of the Bolton Technical College. York's began in Farnworth in the early 20s before expanding into Corporation Street several years later, and Ashley's has fronted the street since the 1930s.

Over the past 50 years there have been many notable occupants of shops in the street, particularly in those facing the Market Hall. A complete list would be far too long and unwieldy. A representative sample would be Redman's Ltd, grocers and dried fruit merchants; Joseph Taylor, house furnisher; Hurst and Nuttall, fish, game and poultry; Lipton's, Blower's and Tate's, grocers; Remelle, fashions; Pearl Radio; Dewhurst's, butchers; Krayson's, footwear; T & M Williams Ltd., wallpaper, paints and decorating materials, and Gray's, furnishers (closed 1980). The Vall-

Bridge Street in 1930. The old Fish Market (demolished 1932/33) made the street exceptionally narrow at its lowest point. On the extreme left is Howard's, tobacconist, and on the right nearest the camera a shoe shop and the Three Tuns Hotel, both of which were demolished in 1957 for extensions to Woolworths. Towering over the Fish Market is the old Flax Mill chimney and on the corner of St George's Road the ornate building which was then occupied by the Bolton Co-op Drapery Department and today houses the Prescription Pricing Authority of the National Health Service.

erina Stocking Bar at one time had over 70 legs in its window, each one encased in a different type of nylon stocking. E Kenyon Ltd. moved to Horwich in 1978, F Steele and Sons, drapers, was taken over by Bolton Co-op in 1955, Duckworth's, lingerie, came into the street from Victoria Square in 1960 and the Salad Bowl has been there for over 20 years.

Corporation Street is not solely a shopping centre. Until recently Corporation House accommodated a multiplicity of offices and other units along its corridors. It now houses the editorial and advertising offices of the Bolton Chronicle, a free newspaper established in the town in March, 1979.

Woolworth's

The site now occupied by Woolworth's was, from 1854 to 1926, owned by leading drapers and funeral directors, Constantine Brothers. Known then as Britannia House, the building took its name from a huge wooden statue of Britannia which occupied a commanding position on top of it. The statue was dismantled and burnt in September, 1942. For 26 years part of Britannia

House was the home of an educational enterprise which, from humble beginnings, culminated in the establishment of the Bolton Technical School. Bolton Mechanics Institute, founded in the 1820s, was sited in the lower section of Richard Constantine's premises (no relation to the later owners of that name) from 1829 until 1855. In the latter year the body transferred to Oxford Street and later to the ornate building at the corner of Mawdsley Street and Bold Street. Here, in 1892, the Mechanics Institute gave way to the Bolton Technical School. These premises now house Bolton Health Studio.

F W Woolworth & Co. began business in Bolton in 1912 at 17-19 Oxford Street, where they remained until they acquired Constantine's premises. Woolworth's formally opened their Deansgate premises on November 27th, 1926, when prices were advertised as "nothing over 6d". This maximum price was to remain for many years. In January, 1957, work started on the demolition of the Three Tuns Hotel, Bridge Street, and an adjoining shoe shop. Both these sites were incorporated into the present Woolworth's building, which was fully opened in

1959.

Mealhouse Lane

That a grain warehouse once stood on, or in close proximity to, Mealhouse Lane to give the thoroughfare its name is undisputed. Messrs Whitehurst certainly had premises on the west side from the 18th to the early 20th century. The name, however, is considered to originate from an earlier business.

The oldest establishment fronting the street today is that which houses the Bolton Evening News offices and departments. This newspaper began on March 19th, 1867, as the brainchild of W F Tillotson and was the first halfpenny evening newspaper unconnected with either a morning or weekly paper, with the exception of a daily "Shipping Gazette" published at South Shields. 40 years later there were no fewer than 106 halfpenny evening newspapers in the U.K.

In its early years the Evening News was printed and published at premises on the corner of Mawdsley Street and Infirmary Street, and a plaque commemorating this fact was unveiled in 1976 on the present-day property on the site. New premises were opened with a frontage to

If a similar shot to this was taken today it would have to be through the glass doors of C & A's store. Since 1957, when the photograph was taken, the section of Chancery Lane in the foreground has disappeared completely along with Ikin's premises on the west side of the street, the whole of the west side of Mealhouse Lane, and the building on the immediate right of the photograph. This was the Queen Anne public house in the 18th century, became the Central Hotel in the late 19th century, and subsequently served several purposes including, from 1946 until 1961, the housing of departments of Tillotsons Newspapers Ltd.

There may be a certain amount of difficulty in equating this scene with that of its modern counterpart. It shows the White Horse Hotel at the Mealhouse Lane/Shipgates corner, one of several properties acquired for extensions to the Bolton Evening News office. These were completed in 1907.

Mealhouse Lane in 1890 and extensions completed in 1907. Tillotsons Newspapers Ltd. became St Regis Newspapers Ltd. in January, 1973, and in January 1982 it was announced that the whole concern had been acquired by Reed International Ltd.

In 1900 the imposing Empress Hall and a new Crown and Cushion public house were erected. The Crown and Cushion closed in March, 1971, and the Empress Hall served the public faithfully as a dance hall for over 65 years before it became the Club Empress and, from February, 1978, Spencer's Club and Bar.

Just over 300 years ago the first non-conformist chapel in Bolton. opened in a house at the corner of Deansgate and Mealhouse Lane. Its founder and first minister was the Rev Richard Goodwin, originally Vicar of Bolton Parish Church but ejected from the living in 1662 under the Act of Uniformity. In 1696 Bank Street Chapel was erected to house the congregation. The Woolpack Inn is subsequently recorded as having occupied the corner site and, after demolition of the remaining vestiges of the old meeting place in the late 19th century, the public house was extended backwards into Mealhouse Lane. The Woolpack closed in 1911 and in February, 1915, the London City and Midland Bank (now Midland Bank Ltd.) opened their new premises on the corner. The bank dates from 1890, when the Preston

Banking Co. Ltd. opened a branch on Bradshawgate between Wood Street and Silverwell Street. Four years later this was taken over by the London and Midland Bank Ltd., which shortly afterwards became the London City and Midland Bank.

National Westminster Bank

The large bank premises on Deansgate between Woolworth's and Wood's Court are in the free Renaissance style, and had their origin in 1836 when the Bank of Bolton began humbly in a small temporary office opening on to Cross Axe Entry, near the present Wood's Court. Its first directors were all men with business interests in the town and district and their names and occupations reflect the principal industries of Bolton at that time. James Rothwell Barnes (cotton spinner), Farnworth; Abraham Haigh (cotton spinner), Bolton-le-Moors; George Lomas (cotton spinner), Farnworth; William Walker (currier), Bolton-le-Moors, John Butler (gentleman), The Haulgh; Thomas Cullen (cotton spinner) and Thomas Ridgeway (bleacher), Wallsuches, Horwich. The bank, and indeed its successors, became known as "The Cotton Bank" and the clue to the nickname lies in the fact that four of the seven directors were prominent local cotton spinning magnates.

Reconstruction work, completed in the latter half of the 19th cent-

ury, necessitated the demolition of the well-known Cross Axes public house, and Cross Axe Entry reverted to its real name of Wood's Court. The licence of the hostelry was transferred to the Globe, later Market Hotel, Ashburner Street.

After being in existence for 60 years, the Bank of Bolton amalgamated with the County Bank Ltd. In 1935 it became the District Bank Ltd. and today it is part of the huge National Westminster group. The present structure was completed early this century to accommodate the business of the old Bank of Bolton and that of the County Bank.

Something of a mystery surrounds part of the present bank's exterior. Over the apex of each of the eight first floor windows facing Deansgate stands a stone head. Who were the persons, part of whose anatomy is immortalised in stone? Do the heads have a symbolic rather than a fully representative function?

Wood's Court

After the demolition of two shops on the east side of Wood's Court earlier this century for extensions to the bank, the present Wood's Court was constructed. For many years the Court led to William Priestley & Co's drysaltery and paint works but today only part of the former works and a rubble-strewn site remain and the Court merely serves as a rear entrance to Woolworth's, the side entrance to the bank and a small car parking area.

To achieve authenticity Wood's Court should really be Woods' Court, for it was named after two members of the Woods family, William Woods and a kinsman, John Woods, who succeeded the former in an ironmonger's shop which occupied the site thereabouts from 1747 to the early 19th century. Wood Street off Bradshawgate also derives its title from the Woods family.

Modelia

The site next to the Old Three Crowns has had a long connection with costumiers and milliners. For over 40 years before the 1950s it was occupied by Messrs Flack's; the fashion house of Modelia has been there since then.

The Old Three Crowns

The 18th century Old Three Crowns had its most recent facelift in 1975, when considerable internal alterations were made to keep the "feel" of the old pub and yet at the same time bring it up to a more tastefully decorated standard.

10 years earlier the gated passageway alongside the hostelry was the subject of a public inquiry, when a Bolton man objected to a proposal by the brewery to close it. He claimed that the path had been used as a public passage for 40 to 50 years. The Corporation denied that the passage was a public right of way and said that it was maintained by its owners, the brewery, who had re-surfaced it. The Ministry of Housing and Local Government subsequently dismissed the Boltonian's appeal.

Martins Bank

Liverpool and Martins Bank Ltd. opened the building at the Crown Street corner in 1925 after occupying temporary offices in Bradshawgate for many years. Later this became just Martins Bank and from 1969 Barclays Bank Ltd.

Crown Street

Crown Street, previously Pepper Alley, is today best known on three accounts – the Old Millstone Inn (at an earlier Millstone Thomas Sharples began a museum and concert hall in 1832, which proved so successful that in 1840 he moved to new premises in Churchgate), Henry Whitehurst and Co., corn merchants, who began in Mealhouse Lane in the 18th century and moved to Crown Street 71 years ago, and Bolton's only multi-storey car park,

which was officially opened in March, 1969.

In July, 1934, the street was the scene of much activity as firemen fought to save one of Bolton's oldest mills from destruction. Their efforts were unfortunately in vain and the Bow Street Mill (Cullen's Mill), tenanted by the African Piassava Co. and Lee's Clog Works, was completely gutted, the fire causing £10,000 damage. On May 1-2, 1961, 19 people lost their lives at the Top Storey Club in the street, in Bolton's worst fire disaster involving loss of life.

Bolton's first Employment Exchange was housed at 9-11, premises now occupied by Laidlaw's.

Whitehead's

Whitehead's, the Fur Store, drapers, milliners, fashions and costumiers, like Whitaker's, is one of the few major independent local businesses to survive the many changes which have taken place over the past 100 years. The store began as a small shop at the corner of Crown Street in 1859. Three adjoining shops on Deansgate were subsequently purchased and in 1909 a new building was erected. To mark the occasion, next-door-but-one neighbours Messrs Preston's supplied 500 solid silver teaspoons and 500 solid silver hatpins and these were given away to customers who spent 20s or over.

In 1912, 4 Deansgate, between the store and Preston's, was acquired

jointly with the jewellery firm and the following year the Deansgate frontages of Whitehead's and Preston's were finally linked together. In 1919 part of Whitehead's was again rebuilt and externally, apart from alterations to the shop windows and further extensions in Crown Street in 1923, the premises have remained to all intents and purposes as they were then.

Preston's

Next door, Preston's Ltd., "The Diamond Centre of the North", is also old-established. Mr John Preston began in a humble way in Hotel Street in the 1860s. Later he transferred to Newport Street and subsequently Bradshawgate before building premises on the present site in 1904. Unfortunately, he was not to see the grandiose terra cotta building which, in conjunction with Whitehead's, the firm opened in 1913. He had died eight years previously.

Many local people, but more particularly visitors to the town, are intrigued by the golden ball which surmounts the top of the building. This, known as a time ball, was erected in 1908 and at 9.00am every day was raised to the top of the guide rods. At exactly 10.00 am, on receipt of a signal from Greenwich, it dropped 10ft to provide an accurate time check. On the occasion of the visit of King George V and Queen Mary to Bolton in July, 1913, it also rendered another public service. It was put into operation the moment the Royal car crossed into west Deansgate and so conveyed the news of the Royal approach to the waiting thousands along the route. The mechanism was discontinued during the Second World War because the weight of the dropping ball threatened damage to the building, and the time ball has never been in action since. Nevertheless, it still provides a prominent local landmark.

Bradshawgate to Mealhouse Lane

Three of the businesses which 50 years ago occupied the stretch between Bradshawgate and Mealhouse Lane are still in existence, although two of them are now in other parts of the town centre. At No. 7 was the True Form Boot Co. Ltd., which is now in Newport Street. At No. 9 Laidlaws, confectioners, occupied premises next door to Crown Entry

Crown Street in May, 1961, the morning after the Top Storey Club fire. The gutted club overlooks the River Croal, and its site and that of adjoining property are incorporated in the huge multi-storey car park.

from the 1880s before moving to Crown Street approximately 12 years ago. The Midland Bank is still at the corner of Mealhouse Lane.

The two longest serving shops at present in the row are both shoe retailers. A Jones Ltd. occupy the corner establishment from which Dean and Dawson, travel agents, operated for many years. Stylo opened their present shop, replacing a smaller one next door, in February, 1960. On the shop's opening the firm claimed it to be the first self-service shoe shop in the North of England. The basement was once the beer cellar of the Joiners Arms public house and the arrangement of barrels and bottles has long since given way to the orderly array of boots, shoes and slippers. The Joiners Arms ("The Big Tub") closed in October, 1958.

There is a tradition that some part of the property entered by the narrow passage known as Crown Entry was held long ago as a nunnery or as an establishment for the dispensation of the Roman Catholic faith.

Schofield's, pork butchers, opened at 21 Deansgate in 1879, and remained there for over 90 years. The shop possessed one of the few private slaughterhouses in the town. The squeals of pigs as they were being led to the slaughter often filled the air in that section of Deansgate and what "fun and games" when one or two escaped and careered along Deansgate and adjoining alleys and streets, hotly pursued by butchers, passers-by and at times members of Her Majesty's constabulary!

The block of property including Schofield's was demolished early in 1970 and the present shop premises constructed. One of the first occupants, taking over from Gingham Kitchen in 1972, was Aristotle's Grill which, from 1961 until 1967, had been Chez Aristotle's in Fold Street.

Bank Street

Bank Street, originally Windy Bank, was undoubtedly one of the earliest and steepest roads leading north out of Bolton.

The building immediately preceding Bank Street Chapel has housed a leather factor's since the 19th century. It was formerly owned by the Hargraves family but since the 1920s has been the property of H Rigby & Co. The present Bank

Street Chapel was built in 1856 but replaced an earlier one erected in 1696. The 100-years-old Sunday School adjoining the chapel was demolished in 1973 and today its site is a pleasant garden and a car park.

Across the road from the Chapel stands the former Villiers Hotel (previously Hare and Hounds). This lost its licence in 1911 and subsequently became a lodging house. Years later the premises were taken over by the Beachcomber Coffee Bar and Disco. Opened in 1963, this subsequently became the Cromwellian Club and the Playmate before assuming a new image and the unusual name of Maxwell's Plum in November, 1977.

At the top of the street, chemical manufacturers Thomas Aspinall wound up in 1975 after 95 years trading in the town. One of the firm's sidelines, a special chemical treatment for fishermen's lines called Mucilin, was very much in demand and exported to nearly every country in the world.

Manor Street

Across the "water" the street becomes Manor Street and although today for all practical purposes Bank Street and Manor Street are one, they were, until the 19th century, in different townships or manors, each with its own governing body. Bank Street still shows a semblance of its former steepness but infilling has considerably reduced the incline. In the case of Manor Street the gradient has been reversed.

One of Bolton's most famous sons, a former Freeman and Mayor of Bolton, the 1st Lord Leverhulme (William Hesketh Lever) began his working life in Manor Street. In 1864 his father, James Lever, purchased a wholesale grocery warehouse "on the right-hand side as one crosses the bridge over the River Croal from Bank Street". Three years later his elder son, William Hesketh, joined the business. Later he left to manage a branch of Lever and Co. in Wigan and during this era decided to specialise in the selling of soap and, shortly afterwards, its manufacture. Subsequently, "Sunlight" soap came on the market and ultimately the works and village at Port Sunlight were erected.

W H Lever was born in Wood Street, Bolton, in September, 1851,

and died as Lord Leverhulme in London in May, 1925. In August, 1981, he was to receive a further commendation when he became the theme of Bolton's second Festival.

At the bottom of Manor Street the Dog and Partridge, at least 140-years-old, changed brewery ownership in 1978 when, after auction by Bass North West, it was purchased by Thwaites'. Its former near neighbour, the Roe Buck Hotel at the junction of Kay Street and Bow Street, had closed in March, 1960, on transfer of its licence to the Prince Rupert Hotel, Holmeswood Road, Great Lever. The building was demolished in February, 1961.

Facing Manor Street from the triangular piece of land between Kay Street and Folds Road, the premises owned by E P Lees Ltd. since 1976 and earlier by Mechanical Services Ltd. were, from 1926 until 1967, a large bakery owned by Bolton Co-operative Society.

Bow Street

Why Bow Street was so called is obscure. T W Sefton, in one of a series of articles under the title "A Local Habitation and a Name" which appeared in the Bolton Evening News in 1934, suggests "it may be that, with the local gaol or dungeon being at the time of naming in the vicinity, in Bank Street, Bow Street was considered an appropriate and metropolitan-sounding name".

Initially, part of the Bow Street site of the present Greater Lancastrian Co-operative Society Ltd. was acquired in 1866 for the princely sum of £310. Five years later the former site of the old Little Bolton Gas Works alongside was purchased. The present offices fronting the street were opened in 1909, the Society's Golden Jubilee Year. Considerable difficulty was experienced during the digging of the foundations, when three old and exceptionally large gas tanks were uncovered. These required excavating and their sites refilling with fresh material. Consequently, building progress was considerably delayed.

All Saints Church, All Saints Street

Today, surrounded by terraced property on one side, old industrial property on two and a corporation car park on another, it is difficult to imagine an earlier church on the same site but in an idyllic rural setting. Yet, that is just what it was.

In 1716 John Moss of Manchester purchased the manor of Little Bolton, then just a fair-sized country estate with a few score of villagers upon its southern boundary. In 1726 he built a chapel for his "manorial dependents", which was appropriately and simply called "Chapel-in-the-Fields". 17 years later the building was consecrated and named All Saints, Little Bolton. The old chapel was demolished in 1869 and the present building opened in 1871. The latter was built from the designs of G E Street (1824-1881), one of the most celebrated Victorian architects and noted for his many English churches in the Gothic Revival style. He also designed the Law Courts in London.

After the closure of All Saints Church in November, 1966, the building was taken over by the Bolton Ukrainian Catholic Church.

River Croal

No mention of Deansgate and adjoining northerly areas can be made without more than a passing reference to the nearby River Croal which, over the centuries, provided a natural steep-sided barrier between them and the countryside to the north and west of the township and between Great and Little Bolton. Rickety wooden bridges which crossed the river at intervals

were replaced in the 19th century by more substantial structures. Knowsley Street bridge, erected in 1852, and Marsden Road in 1877 are examples. Steep slopes were subsequently levelled out and now-adays in several instances, but particularly on Bridge Street, many travellers are unaware that they are crossing a bridge.

That stretch of the River Croal which passes through the town centre belies its name, in that it is really nothing more than a paved stream. The Croal of yesteryear, however, was very different. What can be termed the official history of Bolton, the "Bolton Survey" published in 1953, tells in its opening chapter the whole fascinating story of Bolton in the Ice Age and for a time afterwards. The authors note that "the site of Bolton was determined by the Croal, not the mud-lined stream that one sees creeping along below Queen's Park or in its paved bed shortly after, but a mighty, nameless ancestor, foaming along, with the force of many alpine torrents, and cutting deeply into its bed". A lake, extending far to the south, was formed where Bolton now stands. Into this flowed the gigantic river, depositing its load of sediment, stones, pebbles, sand and mud into the still water. As the great Ice Age passed and the lake dried up, there remained the gravel and sand of the former

delta, which under the Town Hall lies to a depth of about 50 feet.

It is due to the cutting action of this great river and its tributaries, the formation of a delta, ice erosion and earth uplift, that Bolton principally owes its present position, at the convergence of valleys from the north and west. Consequently, the name Bolton is deemed by many to mean "the town (ton) in a bowl (bol)." Another intriguing but less likely definition suggests the name is a contraction of Both-Well-Town, a reference, of course, to the many wells and springs in its vicinity. However, the generally accepted derivation suggests that in its various forms including Bod-elton, Bothelton, Botleton, Boulton, Boulton-super-moras (Bolton-le-moors) to finally just Bolton, the name originates from the Old English and means "a manor house enclosure" or "a place of residence in a bog". Incidentally, the motto under the Bolton Coat of Arms, "Supera Moras", means "Overcome Delays" and is also a pun on the early name of Bolton, Bolton-super-moras i.e. Bolton on the moors.

Rising as the Middlebrook on Red Moss, Horwich, the river changes its name on entering the town in the region of Gilnow. Where exactly the change takes place is not clear and is often debated. The answer would appear to be a classic case of "one pays one's money and takes one's choice". Years ago it was believed that the Croal officially started on the Bolton side of Blackshaw Lane Bridge and an old 1847 map tends to bear this out. More recently a Bolton Corporation official suggested the boundary as being the railway bridge near the Pocket, and the N.W.W.A. (Rivers Division) accepts the Croal as starting at the Park Road/Mayor Street bridge. Does it really matter where the Middlebrook ends and the Croal begins? They are, after all, one and the same watercourse.

In the early 19th century the Croal was a clear, unpolluted waterway flowing between high banks with the houses of the gentlefolk at the top. Gardens and orchards sloped down to the river, which supported trout, dace, gudgeon, eels and pike, and an undated advertisement headed "Bolton-le-Moors, the Garden City of the North" claimed "great attractions" to visitors. Anglers "will find capital sport in the Middlebrook, one of the finest trout streams in the

The case of the expanding foam. A battle for Dr Who against alien beings? No, simply a wall of detergent foam building up after the Middlebrook and part of the Croal had been polluted in 1970. It did, however, cause death and destruction to the fish population of the river. At least 10,000 were estimated to have been poisoned. A Horwich firm was subsequently fined for the offence.

country. There are ample facilities for bathing in the virgin River Croal and swimming competitions are held weekly with the entrance from Water Street and King Street." What a delightful picture the above conjures up and what a contrast to the Croal of today, a rubbish-and-masonry-strewn watercourse flowing between banks of industry and commerce!

By 1859 the offensive condition of the river led to requests that it be paved. The Town Council agreed and work on this between Gilnow Bleachworks and Burnden, apart from a small length alongside Queen's Park, began in 1864 and continued intermittently until completion in 1911. In 1967/8, prior to the construction of St Peter's Way, the Croal was culverted from Church Wharf to beyond Bradford Street.

Thirty years ago pollution was still with us and it was reported to Bolton Town Council that one million gallons of liquid poison were being dumped into the Croal every day and that the fishermen of Bolton were being driven further and further away from the town for a quiet day's sport. By the 1960s the river had become relatively pollution-free and during this decade its lower reaches were restocked with fish. In January, 1970, however, detergent from a Horwich firm swamped the river in foam from Lostock to the town centre and killed an estimated 10,000 fish. 18 months later fish were again seen swimming in the Middlebrook and the Croal, and the Mersey and Weaver River Authority declared the river "clear".

A semblance of the glory of days long gone can still be seen alongside Churchbank. Here, overgrown grassy slopes topped by trees and bushes drop down to a fast flowing stream. Sunshine glints on rippling water and the attractive picture was recently completed when a wild duck and her chick emerged from the dark tunnel under the road and proceeded to swim upstream.

Perhaps in the not too distant future, following more stocking of the river, new plans to cut pollution still further and the Croal/Irwell Valley improvement scheme, the Croal will return to its former glory as a major fishing river, and anglers may yet line its banks or bridges where the river flows through the town centre.

This very old photograph shows the predecessor of the present Parish Church some years before its demolition in 1866. The structure dated from the 15th century and the last service was held in it on April 8th, 1866, when "the crush was so great that there were fears the gallery would break down". The foundation stone of the present St Peter's Church was laid in April of the following year and the building was consecrated in June, 1871.

Churchgate

Although its junction with Bank Street and Bradshawgate is the official start of Deansgate, Churchgate can easily be accepted as an extension of it. Or should Deansgate be classed as an extension of the more historic Churchgate? In any case, no mention of Deansgate is complete without reference to the "continuation" leading to, and alongside, the Parish Church.

50 years ago Churchgate boasted two theatres, a cinema, seven public houses and two temperance bars in its relatively short length. Up to 1962, in fact, the "Gate" was still the entertainment centre of Bolton.

The principal focal point of Churchgate is the Parish Church, that graceful edifice which stands majestically over the Croal Valley and is believed to be the fourth church since Saxon times to have stood on the site. Its predecessor, erected in the 15th century, closed in 1866 and was demolished the same year. The foundation stone of the present church was laid in April, 1867, and the building was consecrated four years later. It cost £45,000 and was paid for by Peter Ormrod, local cotton spinner and banker. The 180ft. tower is claimed to be the highest parish church tower in Lancashire and occupies a somewhat unusual position at the

north-west corner of the church, having been so placed to be a conspicuous object from Deansgate. Incidentally, the four turrets which surmount the tower have names. When the present building was completed, four church officials each lightheartedly named a turret after his eldest child. One was called Percy, another Harriet, a third William and the fourth Cissie.

The number of tunnels reputed to run from the old church to various parts of the town, even as far afield as Deane Church, is legion. One oft-quoted story is that a party of soldiers used a tunnel from the church to escape during the massacre of Bolton in 1644 and there is no doubt that under the Co-op premises in Bridge Street a "tunnel" heads in the general direction of the Parish Church. Years ago, however, after having been explored for a certain distance, the "tunnel" was bricked up at the Bridge Street end and consequently its ultimate destination remains a mystery.

Many so-called "tunnels" discovered today are merely extended cellars of yesterday and the above could fall quite easily into this category. On the other hand, a writer to the Evening News in November, 1966, pointed out that "it is quite correct that some form of arched vault passes beneath Crown Street, Bank Street Chapel and the former Villiers Hotel but it is doubtful that there is any proof or record to show any connection with the old Church of St Peter." He went on to say that "at the rear of Wood's Court there used to be the Bolton Gas Company's No.2 Works and it has often been assumed that the vault was a means of hauling coal from the Manchester-Bolton-Bury Canal wharf to the gas works instead of by horse and cart haulage up the difficult, steep and unpaved slope of Church Bank." Certainly the No. 2 works existed and two of its gas-holders are shown on the 1849 map of Bolton occupying part of the site of the present Co-op premises alongside Bow Street/Bridge Street.

Lengthy cellars, a tunnel once used as an escape route, or a passage used for coal haulage? Perhaps some day excavations during rebuilding will prove which one. Historians and archaeologists deal with facts and not conjectures and would certainly appreciate an authoritative answer. On the other hand, there are many who uphold, and quite rightly, that a mystery solved is a mystery lost and that life will not necessarily be enriched by knowing the answer but will lose a certain "wonderment".

At least one thing is definite. During preparations for the deep foundations required for the present Parish Church, no tunnel entrances were discovered.

Behind the Parish Church, the

building which since September, 1976, has been the parish hall, was for many years a timber store, but from its erection in 1883 until 1899 it was Bolton Grammar School.

Facing the gates to the churchyard stood the old Parish Church Sunday School. Opened in 1819 during the incumbency of Canon Slade (1817-57), the premises at one time housed 1,400 scholars and 110 teachers. The school was extended in 1866 to provide accommodation for the congregation during demolition of the old church and the building of the new one. Demolished in 1972, its site is now occupied by a huge office block, St Peter's House, completed in 1980.

Across Paley Street from the old school stood the Grand Theatre. Opened on August 27th, 1894, it was originally designed as a circus but could be converted in a few hours into a theatre. The circus ring was later built upon. Subsequently, the Grand became one of the foremost music halls in the country. In its heyday a visit "t' Grand" was something to be savoured and the following reminiscence by an obvious devotee, which appeared in the Bolton Journal and Guardian of August, 1975, is suggestive of that certain atmosphere: "I remember the Grand Theatre with people milling about outside the main entrance and the little uniformed attendant shouting 'Booking now for stalls and Grand Circle...' the balcony was just around the

corner. Variety was exactly that in those days, illusionists, balancers, ventriloquists, hypnotists, musical acts of every description, singers, comedians, strong men ... All provided good entertainment and great value for money. Standing in the side street waiting to go in we would be entertained by buskers who went round with a cap. They were very popular in the 30s and played instruments like the piano accordion and the mouth organ. To look after the 'inner man' there were the piemen and the toffee-men, but usually they were exclusive to the balcony patrons. The side door would open and the first house would come out. Then a few minutes later you were running up the stairs with your 6d ready at the cash desk...The safety curtain would slowly rise and the silent adverts would be shown. Joe Hill, the musical director, would appear, the red light blinked and the curtain was up on the first act. All had talent in those golden years..."

The Grand has now departed. It closed in May, 1959, but reopened as the Continental Grand Theatre in December. This closed in July, 1960. The building reopened in June, 1961, as a bingo club and continued as such for 18 months. Along with the Legs of Man and the Derby Arms public houses it was demolished in 1963 and the site is now occupied by a substantial office block.

Adjacent to the Theatre Royal for over 60 years was a building which originally housed the Victoria Theatre of Varieties. This was opened in 1866 on the site of the old Museum and Concert Hall. The building became the Victoria Buffet and finally ceased as a licensed house in 1912. It reopened as the Princess Cinema in 1913 and this in turn became part of the Theatre Royal extensions in 1928.

On January 4th, 1888, fire destroyed the old Theatre Royal but out of the ashes rose a new Theatre Royal, the corner stone of which was laid the following October by the noted actor of the day, Sir Henry Irving. Opened a month later with the play "Hands Across the Sea", it saw many other plays, dramas and musicals enacted on its stage before it was rebuilt on a much grander scale in 1928. Two years later, in January, 1930, it was opened as a "Luxury Talking Picture Theatre", although it had shown films previously. Over the

"Watch the Birdie". Pupils of the former Bolton Grammar School at the rear of the Parish Church pose for a photograph in the school's playground. The old school building was used as a timber yard for 73 years before it was opened as a new parish hall in September, 1976.

ensuing years films alternated with live shows until the showing of the final film, "The Phantom of the Rue Morgue," in February, 1962. The building was demolished, along with the adjoining Bush Hotel, in 1963 and Lennons Supermarket (recently named Foodsave) has occupied the site since.

Bolton Theatre and Entertainments Co. Ltd. was formed in 1889 and over the years controlled the Theatre Royal, the Grand Theatre, the Hippodrome, the Princess Cinema and the Regent, Deane Road. The local Bleakley family had a long association with the company. Alderman James Bleakley (Mayor of Bolton 1942-3) was Managing Director from 1945 to the theatres' demise. His father and grandfather were both connected with the controlling body, his father being Managing Director from 1920 until 1945.

The Grill Olympus opened in 1960. For many years previously it had been the Regent Temperance Bar, better known as "Smokey's" or "Smokey Joe's" on account of its crowded, smoky atmosphere.

The Man and Scythe, the oldest public house in Bolton, was built in 1251 and rebuilt in 1636. A plaque on the front of the building informs us that "in this ancient hostelry James Stanley, 7th Earl of Derby, passed the last few hours of his life previous to his execution Weds 15th October A.D. 1651". The hostelry also bears a crest with its motto "Now Thus Now Thus". The circumstances surrounding the execution and the reason for it are well known but the crest and the motto remain somewhat of a mystery, or rather controversy. At various times they have been claimed by four notable families, the Pilkingtons, the Asshetons, the Bartons and the De Traffords.

It is generally accepted, however, that the Pilkingtons take first place. In his "History of the Pilkington Family of Lancashire...from 1066 to 1600" Lieut-Col. John Pilkington describes the words of the motto as having been the onomatopoeic burden or chorus to a medieval scythe song..."while the illustration is believed to refer to one Leonard Pilkington, who fought at Hastings and after the battle disguised himself as a mower. Both the part-coloured clothes and the words suggest the dual role of knight and mower."

Next door to the Man and Scythe, the Swan Hotel is also an old hostelry. Dating from at least the 17th century it was extensively rebuilt and modernised in 1845, extended and altered in 1930-1 and altered again in 1981. It is not generally realised that the name given to Boltonians, "trotters", is linked particularly with the Swan Hotel. Nothing to do with pigs' trotters, sheep's trotters or trotting races. In former days a person who hoaxed or teased his fellow men was described as indulging in a "trot". On one occasion a Bolton man laid a wager at the Swan that he could endure hotter water than any other man. The wager was taken up and the test was to stand with one foot in a pan of boiling water. The challenger won easily because he had a wooden leg about which he had said nothing. It is reported that the loser, a visitor to the town, paid for the drinks even though he had been "trotted". Boltonians consequently acquired a reputation for "trotting" and became the Bolton Trotters.

The well-known Swan was nearly demoted to a duck in 1972. In that year, new owners wished to rename the hotel the Duck Inn Hotel, but responded to Corporation and public pressure and the Swan was retained in the title.

Churchgate possessed a market cross from 1486 until 1786 and during this period it witnessed many major happenings in the religious and social history of our town – John Wesley spoke there on several occasions, the Civil War raged around it in the 17th century and near it, in October, 1651, the 7th Earl of Derby was executed. Market stalls encroached upon it and the pillory was established thereabouts. The old cross now stands in the grounds of Bolton School. The present obelisk was presented to the town by George Harwood, MP for Bolton from 1895 until 1912, and unveiled on October 16th, 1909. From its 10 ft. diameter base the shaft rises 20ft and work on it was executed at Merrivale Quarries, near Princetown, Devon.

Four bronze shields around its base convey a number of the principal incidents in Bolton's history:-

1253 Bolton a Free Borough by Charter
1256 Charter for market by Henry III to Bodelton (1)
1337 Flemish clothiers settled (2)
1513 "Lusty Lads from Bolton-le-Moors" (Ballad of Battle of Flodden Field)
1540 "Bolton-upon-Moor standeth most by cottons and coarse yarns"(Leland) (3)
1623 Lectureship founded for sermons at Cross
1631 Population 500 (4)
1641 Grammar School Founded (5)
1643-4 During Civil War Bolton besieged thrice and taken once with much slaughter
1651 James seventh Earl of Derby beheaded near this spot
1661 "Bowlton hath a market on Mondays which is very good for clothing and provisions and is a place of great trade for fustians" (Blome's Britannia)
1753 Crompton, inventor of the spinning mule, foundation of modern cotton industry, born in Bolton
1760 Arkwright, founder of the cotton factory system, kept a barber's shop in Bolton
1763 Cotton quiltings and muslins first made at Bolton (6)
1791 Bolton Canal opened
1828 First railway to Bolton opened
1832 First Parliamentary election. Population 41195
1838 Charter of Incorporation
1842 Parliamentary Enquiry about extreme distress in the town
1852 Adoption of Free Libraries Act
1861 Population 70396
1872 First extension of Bolton
1877 Further extension. Population 105214
1898 Bolton again extended
1901 Population 168215

(1) It was in 1251 that Henry III granted a charter for a free warren, a market, and a fair at Bolton

(2) A statement often quoted but according to the "Bolton Survey" 1953 "There is a disputed tradition that some of the Flemish weavers, invited to England under Edward III's Act of 1337, settled in Bolton. Many Flemish weavers settled in East Lancashire about the middle of the 16th century".

(3) 1558

(4) Population probably higher than the figure given.

(5) Grammar School not founded in 1641 but pre-1516. Re-founded in 1657.

(6) Muslins not made locally until the 1780s. Joseph Shaw of Anderton had attempted and failed in 1764 to establish muslin manufacture in the region. Samuel Oldknow commenced manufacture of British muslins at

Anderton in 1783.

Since June, 1933, when the Chief Constable recommended that the cross be removed "in the interest of public safety" there have been suggestions that it be placed in Nelson Square or in the space opposite the Parish Church gates. However, now that Churchgate is partly closed to traffic there is obviously not the same problem and the cross remains on its historic site.

Beswick's shoe shop has attended to the footwear needs of countless people since it was established in Churchgate over a century ago. Recently, it was taken over by another well-known shoe retailer, Nelson's, and renamed Nelson 2. Next door is another well-known and long-standing business, that of Henry Barrie, children's outfitter.

Between Henry Barrie's and the Golden Lion lies the entrance to Gaskell Court, one of Bolton's very few remaining courts. The 400-years-old Gaskell House within its confines was demolished in the 1960s. At the end of the 19th and the beginning of the 20th century it was a place where Mrs Hannah Davis offered "good lodgings". One wonders how many touring theatrical folk playing the Grand or the Theatre Royal took advantage of the facilities offered only a stone's throw from their place of work. In its last years it was the headquarters of the Bolton Chamber of Trade and the Bolton Moral Welfare Association.

Booth's music shop was originally established in Hotel Street in 1832. In 1850 the firm moved to 11, Churchgate and to its present home, No. 17, in 1962.

On the wall of the premises immediately opposite the Man and Scythe, a tablet commemorates the fact that the noted inventor, Sir Richard Arkwright, was once a barber there. Unfortunately, the work in shallow relief and weather-worn is scarcely readable from the street but tells us that "Sir Richard Arkwright, inventor of the water frame for cotton spinning, occupied a shop on this site as a barber and peruke maker from 1760-1768". Even in those days Arkwright was a shrewd businessman and is said to have undercut his competitors by announcing first a shave for 1d. When his colleagues ultimately came down to that price, he went

to ½d. Although there is no firm evidence for the story that one great inventor-to-be used to cut the hair of another, there is no reason why it should not have taken place and it certainly conjures up an interesting picture of the young Samuel Crompton receiving his tonsorial from Arkwright.

Parts of the Golden Lion, now familiarly known as "T'Brass Cat", date back to medieval times. During alterations in the mid-1960s a medieval wall and window were uncovered - the window is thought to be part of a piscina or stone hand basin used in churches. In the second half of the 18th century the licence of the Golden Ball Inn, which stood behind and near Gaskell House, was transferred to the building on Churchgate. From about 1772-78 it was known as the Bear's Paw and in 1779 it was renamed the Crown and Thistle. The name Golden Lion has been associated with the premises since 1806. Earlier this century it was owned by Shaw's brewery, later by Walker's and passed into the hands of the Berni Inns group in 1966, when it was opened as the Golden Lion steakhouse.

The Capitol Cinema, built on the site of old cottages, shops, a billiard hall and a cockpit, was formally opened on February 13th,

1929, and on that day presented two silent films, "Romance" and "Steamboat Bill, Junr." Fifteen months later the Capitol followed the example of several other town cinemas and changed over to talkies. In August, 1962, it was renamed the ABC Cinema and eventually closed in October, 1977. From then until February, 1979, the building housed a bingo and social club. In July, 1980, however, it reopened as a squash club.

One of Bolton's best-known schools of dancing, the Maxwell, moved from upstairs premises alongside the former cinema in August, 1980, to premises in Mawdsley Street.

It is claimed that part of Walsh's Ye Olde Pastie Shoppee dates from the 13th century. Major rebuilding took place in 1667 and it is said that behind the shop in what is now the bakehouse there was a silk mill where child labour was employed.

The Sabinis - Joseph, Andrea and Valentino - opened their ice-cream shop in Churchgate in the 1930s in premises occupied for many years previously by other ice-cream manufacturers - Simonette's, Truffa's, Fielding's and Minion's. In the 1950s the shop underwent a major face-lift, which included a new shop front and ultra modern interior.

Churchgate in 1961. Over the roof of the Derby Arms rises the Grand Theatre. Next door was the Legs of Man and adjoining the Derby Arms the Theatre Royal was showing "A Taste of Love", starring Micheline Presle. Next door stood another of Churchgate's seven hostelries, the Bush Hotel. The Grill Olympus had opened the previous year. Across the street was the Golden Lion in pre-Berni Inn days and the Capitol Cinema had not yet become the ABC Cinema. Incidentally, for film "buffs" the Capitol was showing "Dentist on the Job", starring Bob Monkhouse and Kenneth Connor and "The Man in the Back Seat", with Derren Nesbitt.

Today it bears the title, the Sandwich Inn.

Bolton Area Health Authority has occupied its seven-storey office block at the bottom of Churchgate since 1974. Previously, from 1928, a garage stood on part of the site. The premises demolished to make way for the garage had, from the 17th century to 1887, been the Bolton Parish Church Vicarage.

The Boar's Head, built in 1721, was at that time one of the principal inns of the town. Over the ensuing years it was a Posting House and the meeting place of many former clubs and societies.

Even with all the alterations and additions which have taken place on Churchgate, the "gate" has retained vestiges of its appearance at the turn of the century. The Parish Church towers over its lower reaches. Beswick's (Nelson's) shoes; Booth's, music dealers; the Golden Lion (considerably altered); Ye Olde Pastie Shoppee; the Boar's Head; the Man and Scythe and the Swan Hotel are all still with us.

Before July, 1970, a large volume of traffic made its noisy and reverberating way along Churchgate. In that month and year Church Wharf was severed to allow construction of St Peter's Way. Traffic decreased considerably and even more so with the semi-pedestrianisation of Churchgate itself later the same year.

Churchbank and Church Wharf

Only four premises now remain from over 30 shops and small businesses that existed in Churchbank and Wharf 50 years ago. Gone from Churchbank are several firms which had been there for well over 100 years - Lee's and Rogan's, clog makers and Warr and Co., slate, tile and builder's merchants. Gone also is the Imperial Hotel whilst much earlier, in 1907, the New Bridge Inn at 15 Churchbank closed on transfer of its licence to a rebuilt Crofter's Hotel, St George's Road.

In the 60s the culverting of the Croal and the need for a new major road (St Peter's Way) necessitated the demolition of all that property from the railway bridge to Churchbank. Church Wharf was obliterated. The Bull and Wharf Hotel was demolished in 1966 and within the next few years other property came

The New Bridge Inn, Churchbank, a few years before its licence was removed in 1907 to the Crofter's Hotel, St George's Road. The building, now vacant, is still in existence, the last of the four remaining premises in Churchbank. Wingfield's Silverwell Brewery Co. was sited in Nelson Square, adjoining the Lever's Arms Hotel. It was one of 11 Bolton wholesale breweries which existed at that time, the principal ones being Magee Marshall & Co. Ltd., Crown Brewery, off Derby Street; John Halliwell & Son, Alexandra Brewery, Mount Street; Joseph Sharman, Merehall Brewery, Merehall Street; Spa Wells Brewery Co., Spa Road; and William Tong and Sons Ltd., Diamond Brewery, Deane Road. Bolton's last fully independent brewery, Howcroft's Model Brewery, Spa Road, ceased production in 1969, and the town's last brewery, Magee Marshall's, closed in October, 1970.

down including the Church Wharf Garage; a tobacconist/sweetshop; plumber's premises; Church Wharf Farmhouse (Eckersley's Farm); a saddler's and a herbalist.

Ask most Boltonians why Church Wharf was so called and they would answer that it was the wharf at the Bolton end of the Manchester/Bolton/Bury Canal. This waterway was begun in the 1790s and completed 15 years later. Barges ceased to use it just after the beginning of this century and infilling from Church Wharf began in 1950. Yet an old map predating the canal describes the spot

at the bottom of Churchbank as Church Wharf. Wharth or Warth in this context is now an obsolete word but in the old Oxford English Dictionary it means "a shore, strand; a flat meadow, especially one close to a stream" (the Croal). It was a coincidence that a wharf was later made thereabouts.

Connected with the wharth was the old-established engineering firm of Jackson and Brother Ltd. Today, the practically deserted Wharf Foundry lies just across the Croal. Before the 18th century cotton was bleached by laying the

Only the railway bridge in the background remains from the Church Wharf shown in this 1959 photograph. Constructed for the Bolton-Blackburn line which was opened in 1848, the structure is described by a writer in the Bolton Chronicle of May 27th of that year as "a viaduct of beautiful appearance..." All the property in the foreground was demolished in the 1960s to make way for the Bury New Road extension, opened July, 1970, and St Peter's Way, opened in December, 1971.

cloth in fields or meadows, sprinkling it regularly with clear and pure water obtained from a nearby stream and relying on the action of the sun to bring out the whiteness of the cloth. The area beneath the Parish Church was excellent for this process and an extract from an article on Jackson and Brother which appeared in the journal of the parent company, Mather and Platt group, in 1966, makes interesting reading and reflects the change in use of the old wharth.

"During the latter part of the 18th century chemical processes for carrying out this bleaching were discovered and developed. In Bolton, works were established higher up the Croal, and the chemical waste soon made the water unusable. With natural bleaching thus brought to a sudden end, the owners of the Wharth might well have gone out of business. But they saw in the young chemical bleaching industry an opportunity. Their rivals upstream needed machines.

Putting those Lancashire business heads of their together, the owners of the Wharth decided to go in for the making of bleaching and other textile machinery. And the Wharth was an excellent site. It had the added advantage that the newly-built Manchester to Bolton Canal ended at the edge of the meadow, which meant that coal, pig iron and other supplies could be brought

A section of Church Bank over 50 years ago showing the Imperial Hotel at Nos. 3-5 and Tempest and O'Hara, overall manufacturers, at No. 7. Also on the north side of the "Bank" about this time were the Palatine Window Cleaning and Whitewashing Co.; James Martland, antique dealer; Henry George, confectioner; William Graham, plumber; Jessie Barraclough's boarding house; Rogan's Lion Clog Works, and Arthur Roberts, piano and furniture dealers. The Imperial was one of many Shaw's hostelries taken over by Walker's in 1930.

easily to the works. So the new engineering works came into existence."

Founded in 1792, Jackson's claimed to be the oldest engineering works in Bolton to have remained on its original site and one of the oldest in the country. From the making of bleachworks and textile machinery, the firm ended its days in 1977 specialising in the repair of centrifugal pumps.

The Future

What of the Deansgate of the future? Over 17 years ago Planning Consultant Graeme Shankland suggested that Oxford Street, Victoria Square and Newport Street (north of Great Moor Street) should be made into a pedestrian precinct. He also stated that by 1986 the whole shopping area adjoining and including the main streets could be similarly treated. Since this initial prognosis, Oxford Street, Victoria Square and part of Newport Street have been pedestrianised and Churchgate has been partially closed to traffic.

A scheme is now in the pipeline for a huge shopping complex and multi-storey car park for the area bounded by and including the Market Hall, Knowsley Street, St George's Road and Bridge Street. On the debit side, however, a recent plan to exclude traffic from the part of Deansgate between Bradshawgate and Howell Croft North, with provision for two-way travel for buses, and ultimately to make Deansgate a completely

Looking up the Croal Valley to Church Wharf in 1964. Note the wasteland before the river was culverted in 1967-8. What a contrast to the 1979 photograph (below), which shows the two ribbons of St Peter's Way (opened 1971) sweeping along the valley!

traffic-free precinct was shelved in January 1981 because of the Council's cash shortage. The whole idea initially hinged on the construction of the northern and southern limbs of the inner relief road and a major traffic reorganisation scheme. The southern limb was opened in 1979 and the northern limb in January 1982.

Let us hope that the intended plan will not now be lost in the mists of time. Planners certainly believe that the envisioned scheme will make the town even more attractive to shoppers. So it will, but a prime requisite for any success, for both shoppers and retailers, will be the provision of adequate and adjacent car parks, bus stops and bus stations. The three major subjects of this book will thrive commercially but only if the public transport situation is resolved. Again, Shankland

Graeme Shankland's futuristic Deansgate looking towards his new 'town square' at the convergence of the thoroughfare with Oxford Street and Knowsley Street.

suggested, and made provision for, up to 10,000 free car spaces within the inner relief road area. From these there should be easy access for passengers to and from the central shopping area. For those not in their own transport, two bus interchanges were proposed and frequent bus stops along a circular route.

All being well, we may yet see a tree-lined, inner core shopping centre with passenger-carrying, silent, electric "donkeys" threading their way carefully through crowds thronging a shopper's paradise.

APPENDIX 1

Public houses, inns and hotels in Deansgate, Churchgate, Churchbank and Victoria Square closed from 1879 to date.

(D) = Deansgate (C)=Churchgate (CB)= Churchbank (V)=Victoria Square

Angel Inn (C) see Victoria Buffet

Bay Horse (D) "Scotch Vaults" – acquired by Marks & Spencer in June, 1959, licence surrendered in April, 1960, and the building subsequently demolished to make way for the new Marks & Spencer's store.

Bee Hive (D) – demolished c1900 for Deansgate widening scheme and licence allowed to lapse. Former Head Post Office erected on site.

Bush Hotel (C) – formerly Star Inn – demolished in 1963 along with the Theatre Royal. Site now occupied by Lennon's Supermarket (Foodsave).

Coach and Horses (D) – compensated 1907. Site now part of Y.M.C.A. and shop property.

Commercial Hotel (V) – closed April, 1972, and demolished in November of that year to make way for new Mothercare store.

Concert Tavern (C) – closed for extension to Grand Theatre in 1909.

Cross Axes, Wood's Court (D) – licence removed to Globe, later Market Hotel, Ashburner Street, 1879. Premises demolished for extension to County Bank (now National Westminster Bank).

Derby Arms (C) – demolished, along with Grand Theatre, in 1963. Site now occupied by Churchgate House.

Four Horse Shoes (D) see Silver Vat

Fox and Goose (D) – licence renewal refused and premises pulled down for erection of Fire Station (now Marsden House) in 1897.

Grapes Hotel (V) – licensed 1840 – demolished 1959 for town centre redevelopment.

Hand and Banner (D) – closed 1911. Site now part of Lloyds Bank Chambers.

Higher Nag's Head Hotel (D) also known as "Holden's Vaults". Closed July, 1929, and demolished in March, 1930, to make way for tailoring premises.

"Holden's Vaults" see Higher Nag's Head.

Imperial Hotel (CB) earlier Rising Sun – closed 1934 on transfer of licence to King's Arms Hotel, Chorley Old Road. Became

guest house before demolition at the end of the 1960s to make way for new office block.

Joiner's Arms (D) – closed October, 1958. Site now shop property.

Jones' Hotel (D) see Rose and Crown

King's Arms (D) – closed March, 1962. From 1974–80 Chapter and Verse Bookshop and from December, 1980 to date Sweetens booksellers.

King's Head (D) – demolished in 1969 to make way for the widening of Blackhorse Street

Legs of Man (C) – demolished 1963. Site now occupied by Churchgate House.

Lion's Paw (D) see Silver Vat

Lord Collingwood (D) – licence transferred July, 1894, to Oddfellow's Arms, St Helens Road. Shop premises on site.

New Bridge Inn (CB) – licence surrendered 1907 on grant of licence to Crofters, St George's Road. Premises still there.

Old Hen and Chickens (D) – licence transferred to Railway Shipping Inn (later Brunswick Hotel) August, 1888. Site now occupied by Podmore's.

Queen's Arms (D) – closed 1907. Site now occupied by part of Y.M.C.A. and shop premises.

Red Lion (D) official address, 29, The Shambles, Deansgate – licence transferred to Tramways Hotel, Blackburn Road 1881.

Rising Sun (CB) see Imperial Hotel

Rope and Anchor (D) – closed 1899 on removal of licence to Halliwell Lodge Hotel. Property demolished for widening of Bridge Street.

Rose and Crown (D) – Just prior to closure known as Jones' Hotel – licence transferred to Railway Hotel, St Helens Road, 1884. Building demolished to make way for shop premises.

"Scotch Vaults" (D) see Bay Horse

Silver Vat (D) – originally the Four Horse Shoes then the Lion's Paw and, after rebuilding in 1907, the Silver Vat. Closed 1927 when its licence was transferred to the Bowling Green, Bury Road. Parr's Bank (now National Westminster) extended to occupy the whole corner from Oxford Street to Old Hall Street North.

Star Inn (C) see Bush Hotel

Town Hall Hotel (V) Old Hall Street South/ Victoria Square corner – closed February, 1933. Premises demolished for Corporation improvements 1947.

Town Hall Tavern (V) – closed 1925. Site now occupied by Magistrate's Court Dept., Le Mans Crescent.

Victoria Buffet (C) previously Angel Inn – closed December, 1912. Became Princess Cinema before being incorporated into Theatre Royal extension in 1928. Theatre Royal demolished 1963.

Welcome Home (D) – demolished c1900 for Deansgate widening scheme and licence allowed to lapse. Former Head Post Office erected on site.

White Bear Inn (D) – most of the hostelry was sited alongside Crown Entry – licence transferred 1880 to Bradford Hotel, Bradford Street.

Woolpack (D) – closed 1911. Site now occupied by Midland Bank Ltd.

APPENDIX 2
Deansgate

as detailed in Tillotsons Bolton Directory, 1932

BRADSHAWGATE here
Dean & Dawson Ltd, tourist agents
Greenhalgh Hugh & Co Ltd, dyers & cleaners
Lancs & Cheshire Rubber Co, rubber merchants
True Form Boot Co Ltd, boot salesmen
CROWN ENTRY here
Laidlaw Ltd, confectioners
Scotts Ltd, tailors
Maypole Dairy Co Ltd, tea and butter merchants
Williams (Bolton) Ltd, wholesale and retail glass, china and earthenware factors
Joiners Arms
Playfair Henry Ltd, boot and shoe dealers
Lavell's confectioners
Schofield Mark, provision merchant and pork butcher
Harris John, clothier and tailor
Midland Bank Ltd
MEALHOUSE LANE here
Dunn G A & Co, hat specialists
Bay Horse
Dees, confectioners
Talbots (Confectioners) Ltd, caterers
Marks & Spencer Ltd, multiple stores and bazaar
Lower Nag's Head Hotel
Burton Montague Ltd, tailors
MARKET STREET here
Union Bank of Manchester Ltd
Vickers Norman, gent's tailor, Union Bank Chambers
Smith & Gregson, colliery agents, Union Bank Chambers
Weaver to Wearer Ltd, tailors
Vose & Son, tripe dealers
OXFORD STREET here
Westminster Bank Ltd
OLD HALL STREET NORTH here
Whitakers (Bolton) Ltd, The Departmental Store, fancy drapers, etc.
Aspinalls Ltd, pork butchers
Batten George, glass and china dealers
Ellwood R, silk specialist
Smiths (Bolton) Ltd, milliners and gown specialists
Jacksons Ltd, hat and boot specialists
Aspin Hall: First Church of Christ Scientist
HOWELL CROFT NORTH here
SPRING GARDENS here
BACK SPRING GARDENS here
Lloyds Bank Ltd
Taylor Gilbert, boy's outfitter, Lloyd's Bank Chambers
McLeod J S & Co Ltd, electrical and radio engineers, Lloyd's Bank Chambers
Thornley John & Son, auctioneers and valuers, Lloyd's Bank Chambers
Huddersfield Building Society, Lloyd's Bank Chambers
Steele M, milliner, Lloyd's Bank Chambers
Kemp W W, solicitor, Lloyd's Bank Chambers
Christian Alliance: Woman and Girls' Pioneer Club and Cafe, Lloyd's Bank Chambers
Hart James and Sons, pork butchers
Stuttard & Whitworth, modistes
Y.M.C.A.
Bolton Boys' Federation (headquarters)
Mawdsley Street Congregational P.S.A. Institute
Burgons Ltd, grocers and provision dealers
West Riding Wallpaper Co, wallpaper dealers
Sharples', cabinet makers

Longworth W & A, confectioners
QUEEN STREET here
Hippodrome
BACK QUEEN STREET here
Hen and Chickens
King's Head Hotel
Wright Miss Kate, confectioner
BLACKHORSE STREET here
Sanderson William, grocer and confectioner
Margiotta Herbert, tobacconist
Vinten Miss Maud E, grocer
Swain Wilfred, fried fish dealer
Sharples William H, newsagent and tobacconist
BACK BLACKHORSE STREET here
White Lion Hotel
MOOR LANE here
SPA ROAD here
Ritherdon & Co Ltd, electroplaters and enamellers, North Bridge Mill (yard)
Gipsy's Tent
MARSDEN ROAD here
Beau Brummel (1928) Ltd, dyers, cleaners and valet service
Gordons, motor dealers, authorised Ford dealers
ST EDMUND STREET here
Tognarelli's Ltd, cafe
Swift Eugene N, chemist and photographic dealer
Heeley Percy, grocer and confectioner
Greyhound Inn
BACK KING STREET here
Beardsworth Geo., hairdresser
Beardsworth Miss Mary A, newsagent and tobacconist
Seddon Frank, grocer
Knowles Herbert, grocer
Hart John, butcher
Thomas John & Sons, boot and clog makers
KING STREET here
Head Post Office
Dewhirst & Co, tailors and clothiers
Smith Maison, ladies' and gent's hairdresser
Pare H B & Co, chemists and photographic dealers
Bolton Workers' Sports Club
Communist Party of Great Britain, Minority Movement
Cowbourne Frank, tailor
Modern School of Dancing
Smith Miss Annie, milliner, The Regent
Joyce, ladies' and children's hairdressers, Bradley's Chambers
Bolton & District Regional Town Planning Committee, Bradley's Chambers
Bradley Walter (Eng.) Ltd, motor engineers, etc.
CENTRAL STREET here
Rowley & Co, opticians
Winterburn G, bookseller, stationer, newsagent, ordinance map agent
Blue Boar Hotel
CHAPEL ALLEY here
Thornton & Co, jewellers
Spibey W, fruiterer and florist
Wolstencroft Mrs A, grocer
Podmore's, seed and bulb importers
Tognarelli, confectioner
Kings Arms
Hampsons (Bolton) Ltd, confectioners
Crook Edward, fish and game salesman
RIDGWAY GATES here
Stewarts (Clothiers), Ltd, tailors
Dolcis Shoe Co, boot and shoe dealers
Redhead's, silk mercers and general drapers, The Silk Store
KNOWSLEY STREET here
Dodgson Henry, Ltd, costumiers and furriers
Barratt W & Co Ltd, boot and shoe makers
Smith, Walter & Co Ltd, piano and gramophone dealers
MILLWELL LANE here
Bolton Co-operative Society Ltd, Jewellery Department
MARKET STREET here
Williams Deacon's Bank Ltd
Bank House
Seymour Mead T & Co Ltd, provision merchants and caterers
Graveson George & Sons, builders' furnishing ironmongers
Taylor Harry S, jeweller and silversmith
Imperial Playhouse
Roberts & Co, raincoats and mantles
BRIDGE STREET here
Woolworths F W & Co Ltd, departmental stores and bazaar
The County Bank (Manchester and County Bank, Ltd)
Bank Caretaker
Priestley W & Co, drysalters, oil refiners, colour and varnish merchants
WOOD'S COURT here
Flacks H Ltd, costumiers and milliners
BACK CROWN STREET here
Old Three Crowns
Martins Bank Ltd
CROWN STREET here
Whitehead R & Son Ltd, drapers, ladies' tailors, furriers, milliners and costumiers, The Fur Store
Prestons Ltd, watchmakers, jewellers and silversmiths
BANK STREET here

Victoria Square

as detailed in Tillotsons Bolton Directory, 1932

MARKET STREET and HOTEL STREET here
Ross Munro & Co Ltd, wine and spirit merchants
Taylor Mrs Gertrude, costumier and ladies' outfitter
Cook Thomas & Son Ltd, tourist agents
Laidlaws Ltd, confectioners
Lythgoe W R Ltd, wholesale and retail confectioners
Ribble Motor Services Ltd
Alston William J, grocer
Harts, household linen stores
Hyde Bros., milliners and fancy drapers
Hindle Thomas E, wholesale hardware & smallware dealer
Bulloughs W (Confectioner) Ltd, confectioners
Ideal Cleaners & Dyers Ltd
EXCHANGE STREET here
Grapes Hotel
Back CHEAPSIDE here
Bolton Public and Reference Library
NEWPORT STREET here
Manchester Furnishing Warehouse, house furnishers
Borough Engineers' Dept.
Wood & Co, tea & coffee merchants
Leach Ernest, health food stores
Lancashire Wallpaper Co, decorators' merchants
OLD HALL STREET SOUTH here
Public Lending Library
HOWELL CROFT SOUTH here
Christy Arthur, motor coach proprietor
HOWELL CROFT NORTH and OLD HALL STREET NORTH here
OXFORD STREET here
Commercial Hotel

Churchgate

as detailed in Tillotsons Bolton Directory, 1932

United Cattle Products Ltd, wholesale and retail tripe dressers
Beswick Charles H, footwear dealer
Proffitt John, costumier and milliner
Winder & Winder, window sign manufacturers
Greenhalgh Peter & Gregson, incorporated insurance brokers
Stringfellow F M & H, woollen and trimming dealers
Women's Citizens Association (Mary Haslam Centre)
Girl Guides Headquarters
Booths, musical dealers and repairers
Golden Lion
Gent Miss Annie Lilian, confectioner
Lingard Joseph, cycle dealer
Gent Mrs Sarah E, temperance bar and tobbacconist
Capitol Picturedrome
Roberts Arthur, furniture dealer
Walsh Mrs Ida, confectioner
Royal Confectionery Co, wholesale confectioners
Senior H & S, ladies' and gentlemen's tailors and raincoat specialists
(back) Tasker Fredk. constructional engineer
Thomasson Edith, newsagent and tobacconist
Boar's Head
Hill Fred., chimney sweeper
Crook John (Bolton) Ltd, ornamental ironwork and heating engineers
Bolton Lead Works Co Ltd, lead pipe manufacturers
Fletcher John, motor engineers, garage
Jarrold Alfred, fried fish dealer
Rogers Edward, window cleaner
Jones Alice, boarding house keeper
Jackson Mrs Ann, boarding house keeper
St Peter's Parish Church and Schools
School House
Grand Theatre
Legs of Man
Derby Arms Hotel
Theatre Royal Picture Palace
Bush Hotel
Hawkins Mrs Louisa A, temperance bar
Man and Scythe
Swan Hotel

Deansgate

as at January 1st 1982

A Jones & Sons, footwear
Fashion Wagon, discount menswear
Magna Carta, male fashions
CROWN ENTRY here
Anglo Continental Travel, travel agents
Terry's Ring Room, jewellers
Stylo, footwear
Visionhire, television rental
Aristotle's Grill restaurant
Eric Slinn, wallpapers and paints
Bolton Camera Centre
Midland Bank
MEALHOUSE LANE here
Marks & Spencer
Dunn & Co, tailors
Lower Nag's Head Hotel
Hepworths, tailors
Burton, tailors
MARKET STREET here
Barclays Bank
Pizzaland Restaurant
Dixons Cameras
Ratners, jewellers
OXFORD STREET here
National Westminster Bank
OLD HALL STREET NORTH here
Whitakers
Health Food Store
Whitakers
Gibson's Sports
Famous Seconds shop
Whitakers
HOWELL CROFT NORTH here
Lloyds Bank
Lloyds Bank Chambers

- 1st Floor
  Hushon-Brown (Electrolysis and Beauty
     Clinic)
  J Esner & Co, solicitors
- 2nd Floor
  Bolton & District Textile Employers
     Association
Deansgate Discount
Cyril Hough, butcher
Greenhalghs, bakers
Save the Children second hand shop
Y.M.C.A.
Y.M.C.A. Youth Dept. coffee bar
The Deansgate Pharmacy Ltd
Littles Hair Salon
And So to Bed, bed sales
   - Original Pine Emporium, restored pine
        furniture
Spencers, dyers and cleaners
     QUEEN STREET here
Deansgate Health Centre (entrance in
     Queen Street
     BACK QUEEN STREET here
Hen and Chickens
     BLACKHORSE STREET here
Bromley, optician
vacant property
The Joke Shop
West End Chip Restaurant
vacant property
     BACK BLACKHORSE STREET here
White Lion Hotel
     MOOR LANE here
     SPA ROAD here
Gipsy's Tent
     MARSDEN ROAD here
Social Services Dept., Marsden House
     ST EDMUND STREET here
Leyland, wallcoverings and paints
Pedigree Dog Shop
The Greyhound
     BACK KING STREET here
Newsagent
M Boyd, tailoring specialist
Cut Price cosmetics
The Bigger Barmcake, take-away sandwich
     bar
Manchester Warehouse Ltd, furniture
     KING STREET here
former Head Post Office building
     KINGSGATE here
SupaSnaps, film developing and printing
Whittakers, The Shoemakers
Cane Country
   - Michael Gildea, hair salon
Hitchens Clearance Store
     CENTRAL STREET here
Rowley, optician
West End Newsagency
Blue Boar
     CHAPEL ALLEY here
vacant premises (to be opened shortly as
     Greenhalgh's craft bakery)
Gibson's Sports
Podmore Ltd, garden centre
C Cheadle & Sons, confectioners
Sweetens, booksellers
Hampsons, bakers
Cafe and snack bar
     RIDGWAY GATES here
Coombes, shoe repairers
Cut Price Stores
Deansgate Distribution Ltd, discount store
     KNOWSLEY STREET
John Collier, tailors
Wimpy Bar
H Samuel, jewellers
     MILLWELL LANE here
Harris Carpets
     MARKET STREET here
Williams and Glyn's Bank
New Day, furnishing
Allied Carpets
Boots, chemist
     BRIDGE STREET HERE

F W Woolworth & Co Ltd
National Westminster Bank
     WOOD'S COURT here
Modelia, fashions
Old Three Crowns
Barclays Bank
     CROWN STREET here
Whiteheads, drapers, etc
Prestons, jewellers
     BANK STREET here

Victoria Square

as at January 1st 1982

     HOTEL STREET here
Boots, chemists
W H Smith, booksellers and stationers
British Home Stores
Hames (Hagenbachs) the Bakers
Saxone, shoe retailers
Conley's jewellers
Thomas Cook, travel agents
Woodhouse, furniture
     EXCHANGE STREET here
DER, television rentals
Wimpy, snack bar
     BACK CHEAPSIDE here
Nationwide Building Society
     NEWPORT STREET here
Halfords, car and cycle accessories
North West Gas showroom and offices
     OLD HALL STREET SOUTH here
Bolton Public Libraries Dept. Bibliographic
     Services Unit
     HOWELL CROFT SOUTH here
     LE MANS CRESCENT here
     HOWELL CROFT NORTH here
Paderborn House
   - Head Post Office
   - Local Government Offices, etc.
     OLD HALL STREET NORTH here
Co-op Department Store
     OXFORD STREET here
Mothercare Store
     MARKET STREET here

Churchgate

as at January 1st 1982

     BANK STREET here
Susan Smart, milliners
Nelson 2, shoes
Henry Barrie, children's wear
     GASKELL COURT here
   - Bolton Dental Laboratories
Golden Lion, restaurant and bar
sweets and tobacco
Booths, music
Ace Travel
JJB Sports: Bolton Squash Club
Hilary Anns, fashions
Walsh's pies and pasties
Sandwich Inn
The Chip Inn, fish and chips
Boars Head
Gatehouse cafe and take-away
Bolton Area Health Authority headquarters
Capitol House
   - Mercantile Credit Co Ltd
   - Keepsake Perfumes
   - Keepsake Jewel Case Co Ltd
   - Prestons Timber Division
   - Northern Bureau of Defaulters
   - Lloyds and Scottish Finance Ltd
   - Datsun Finance Ltd
   - Auto Union Finance Ltd
   - Billington Bros. (Wombwell) Ltd
   - Northern Design and Detail
     (Structural) Ltd
     CHURCHBANK here
     SILVERWELL LANE here
St Peter's House
   - Telebank
     PALEY STREET here
Carlton, Kirkpatrick & Co

Harker & Howarth Sound Centre
Harker & Howarth Music Dept.
Bolton Sports Centre
Lennons wine shop
North Fur Co.
Churchgate House
     -Wesleyan and General Insurance
     - Burroughs Machines Ltd
     - Knitting Lace & Nat. Industry
        Training Board
     - South Lancashire Knitting Industry
        Training Group
     - Federated Insurance Co Ltd
     - Illingworth and Henriques, stock-
        brokers
     -Churchgate Financial Administration
        Ltd, financial consultants
     - Kingsley Associates, architects
     - Robert Spencer Ltd
     - Guardian Royal Exchange Assurance
        Ltd
     - Guardian Assurance Co Ltd
     - MacMillan Bloedel Meyer Ltd
     - Douglas A Haslam, solicitor
     - Cyril Morris, Arkwright & Co,
        solicitors
     - Churchgate House Nominees Ltd
     - Manpower Services Commission
        Training Services Division
Lennons Supermarkets Ltd
Grill Olympus
Man & Scythe
Swan Hotel
     BRADSHAWGATE here

Acknowledgements

I am indebted to Mr Leslie Gent,
Editor of the Bolton Evening News,
for his permission to reproduce all
the photographs used except for
those of the Black Horse Hotel,
Grapes Hotel, Imperial Hotel and
King's Head Hotel, which were
kindly loaned to me by Mr Neil
Richardson.

My thanks to local historians of
the past and present, relatives,
friends, colleagues and acquaint-
ances who, over the years, have
provided me with items of inform-
ation without which this work could
never have been compiled.

Special thanks to the late Harry
Greenhalgh, a member of the Bolton
Industrial History Society, and Mr
W E Brown, M.A., Vice-Chairman
of the Bolton Civic Trust, for advice
on, and correction of, many historical items, and to Mr Brown for the
provision of an excellent foreword.